The Early Gravestones of Killingworth

Gravestone of Eli Kelcey, 1788, Southwest District Cemetery, Killingworth

The Early Gravestones of a Colonial Town: Killingworth, Connecticut

Thomas L. Lentz

The Killingworth Historical Society

2019

Library of Congress Control Number: 2019900231

ISBN 978-1-937721-67-1

Produced by Peter E. Randall Publisher, Portsmouth, NH 03802-4726

Rite bleſsed are the dead
That die In the LORD

Captain Ebenezer Redfield gravestone, 1766

Contents

Introduction

This book documents and photographically records gravestones in Killingworth, Connecticut. The majority of stones depicted are in present Killingworth. Killingworth, however, once included present Killingworth and the town of Clinton to the south, and was settled as the Plantation of Hammonasset in 1663. Thus, some gravestones including the earliest in Clinton are included. In addition, a portion of Durham was once a part of Killingworth and some stones in Durham are shown when they have a relationship to Killingworth or illustrate noteworthy stylistic features.

The book has several purposes. First and foremost is to preserve images of the remaining early gravestones in Killingworth. Large numbers of stones have already deteriorated beyond recognition or are broken or buried. Many others are in precarious condition. The book does not illustrate all of the markers in Killingworth, there are thousands, but it does include virtually all of the eighteenth century gneiss and sandstone gravestones that are intact and have readable inscriptions. Second, Killingworth gravestones have been almost totally overlooked in books on gravestones. The Farber Collection, which includes over 2,000 photographs of Connecticut gravestones, has only six from Killingworth and Clinton. The reasons for this are uncertain; perhaps Killingworth was viewed as too provincial and rural to have any significant stones. Some of the books tend to concentrate on elaborately styled gravestones such as found in the Boston area. As will be seen, though, Killingworth has many noteworthy stones. There are also many relatively plain and simple stones, and these are included as well to illustrate the entire range of styles of stones in the area. It is hoped that these photographs will fill a regional gap that will be useful to future researchers and scholars of gravestones. Thirdly, the Rev. William Seward, pastor in Killingworth from 1738 to 1782, did not record deaths in the church records. As a result, dates of death for Killingworth residents during this period are not present in the Barbour Collection of Vital Statistics for Connecticut. For genealogists, the inscriptions on the gravestones are the only remaining record. Finally, it is hoped the book will increase awareness of the artistic and historic significance of gravestones and encourage public efforts to preserve them.

Special thanks are due to Professor Jelle Zeilinga de Boer who educated the author on the mineral composition of gravestones. Jeff Klausen and Eamonn Smith provided the muscle power to reset many fallen gravestones. Members of the Killingworth Historical Society and others have worked to clean and reset gravestones and to cut brush in the old graveyards.

All profits from the sale of this book go to the support of the Killingworth Historical Society and its preservation efforts.

Thomas L. Lentz
Killingworth Municipal Historian
Killingworth, Connecticut 2019

The History of Killingworth

Killingworth originally comprised present day Killingworth and the Town of Clinton to the south. Killingworth was first settled in 1663 as the Plantation of "Homonoscitt" (Hammonasset), located on the Connecticut shore between Saybrook and Guilford. Among the regulations for the ordering of the plantation in October 1663 was that there shall be at least thirty families on the east side of the Hammonasset River. The 30 lots were laid out along what is Main Street in Clinton on both sides of the Indian River. Then, at a Court of Election held in Hartford on May 9, 1667, it was ordered that "ye towne of Homonoscit shal for ye future be named Kenilworth, & for y^{r} brand of horses they shal have ye letter V on ye near buttock." On October 10, 1667, the Court gave permission for the inhabitants of Kenilworth "to gather themselves into church order." In October 1667, a call to be minister was made to the Rev. John Woodbridge, a graduate of Harvard College. He was pastor until 1679 when he resigned and became pastor in Wethersfield, Connecticut. Through corruption of spelling, Kenilworth became Killingworth, which was used exclusively after 1707.

At the time of settlement, the Native Americans in this region were the Hammonassets who lived along the shore between the Aigicomock, now East River, and the Connecticut River. They were a peaceful tribe and left behind their burial grounds and large mounds of shells. The name of their Sachem was Sebaquaneh or "the man that weeps." Uncas, Sachem of the Mohegan, married his daughter and came into possession of the lands of the Hammonassets. On the 26th of November, 1669, Uncas, with Joshuah, his son, sold to the inhabitants of Killingworth all the lands in the township, which he had not sold before to George Fenwick, Esq. of Saybrook. They reserved for themselves "Six acres of Land on the Great Hammock." An Indian village in present Killingworth was located about 0.4 mile north of Route 80 and in the vicinity of the junction of Roast Meat Hill Road and the abandoned Wolf Meadow Road. There are a few rock shelter sites in Killingworth where Indian artifacts have been found.

The following names of settlers are listed in the Killingworth town records: "The Names of the Planters admitted by the Committee & now settled in the place & others by the Company admitted as now Stand on Record are – December 28 – 1665 -."

1. Byran Rossetter
2. William Haydon
3. Edward Griswold
4. John Miegs Senr
5. Josias Hull Senr
6. William Kelcey
7. William Wellman
8. Samuel Buell
9. Jonas Westover
10. William Barber
11. Mr Matthew Allyn
12. Joseph Wilkison
13. Thomas Smith
14. Henry Farnam
15. John Rossetter
16. Jonathan Dunnin
17. Thomas Steevens
18. William Steevens
19. George Chatfield
20. John Kelcey
21. Henry Crane
22. Eleazer Isbel
23. Benjamin Wright
24. Joseph Hand
25. Robert Williams
26. John Nettleton
27. John Hodge
28. Josiah Hull Senr
29. Parsonage Lot
30. Minister's first Lot"

The town grew slowly at first. The original settlers were followed by Nathaniel Chittenden, Daniell Clark, Robert Lane, Nathaniell Parmelee, Edward Rutty, Ananias Turner, Christopher Tooley, and Andrew Ward. Many of these family names will be seen on the gravestones to follow. In 1686, there were 36 persons (freemen only were counted) living in town and a list of 2412 pounds. By 1706, there were 63 persons and a list of slightly over 3391 pounds. The descendants of many of the original settlers later moved to the northern part of the town. On several occasions, the Town of Saybrook made claims on land in Killingworth. The dispute was finally settled in 1687/8 when 31 Killingworth planters paid Saybrook £30 for "right of soil." Finally in 1718, a joint committee of the two towns agreed on a straight line dividing the two towns. In October 1703, a patent or act of incorporation was granted by the General Assembly to the proprietors and inhabitants of "Kilinworth" giving them rights to the land and establishing the bounds of the town.

The Rev. Abraham Pierson was called as pastor in 1694. He was highly respected by the townspeople. He also holds the distinction of being the first Rector or president of what was to become Yale College and held the first classes in Killingworth. His house was located in Clinton near where the Stanton house now stands. Pierson was one of ten prominent ministers in Connecticut who were named to stand as Trustees or Undertakers to found, erect, and govern a College in the Colony of Connecticut. On October 9, 1701, the General Assembly granted unto the Undertakers "full Liberty, Right, and Privilege" to erect and form a Collegiate School. The Trustees then chose the Rev. Mr. Abraham Pierson "to take the Care of Instructing and Governing the Collegiate School; under the Title and Character of RECTOR." They also chose Saybrook as the most convenient place to "erect and fix the Collegiate School." They desired the Rector to move to Saybrook but until that could be accomplished ordered that the Scholars should be instructed at or near the Rector's house in Killingworth. Eight students, some of whom had been studying privately with one or another of the Trustees, were admitted. The first Commencement was held at the house of the Rev. Mr. Thomas Buckingham at Saybrook on September 13, 1702. The Trustees continued in their efforts to remove the Rev. Pierson to Saybrook and offered significant financial inducements. However, the people of Killingworth strongly opposed this so that the students continued to study with the Rev. Pierson in Killingworth until his death in 1707. Mr. Pierson on his deathbed advised those present to select Mr. Jared Eliot, one of his students, as his successor as pastor.

The Rev. Jared Eliot, one of Pierson's pupils and a graduate of the Collegiate School in 1706, preached for about two years and was called as pastor and ordained on October 26, 1709. He was the son of the Rev. Joseph Eliot, pastor in Guilford, and a grandson of John Eliot, the celebrated apostle to the Indians of New England. He served as minister for 54 years. In addition, he was a distinguished physician and scientist. He was a friend of Benjamin Franklin who visited him occasionally. He was also a botanist and agriculturist, and introduced the white mulberry tree and the silkworm to Connecticut. He operated the iron forge off Ironworks Road in present Killingworth, an important forge in colonial times. The forge supplied steel for Connecticut and other colonies used for the manufacture of armaments in the Revolution.

Killingworth at one time included part of what is now Durham to the north. Durham was a tract of land called Coginchaug located between Middletown on the north, Haddam on the east, Killingworth and Guilford on the south, and Wallingford on the west. In the seventeenth century, the General Court of the Colony granted tracts of land in Coginchaug to distinguished men for civil, military, and ecclesiastical services. One recipient of a grant of 100 acres was the Rev. Abraham Pierson of Killingworth. In 1686, the Court granted the southeastern part of the territory to Killingworth. "This Court grants to the towne of Kenilworth all those lands of the north of their bownds and Guilford, and the west of Haddum bounds up to Cawgenchaug swamp, which are not formerly granted to any Township or particular person." The first settler in Durham was Caleb Seward, a tanner from Guilford. He settled in 1699 and was followed by his brother Joseph Seward, a physician, and nephews John Seward and William Seward. Deacon William Seward (1684–1764) was the father of the Rev. William Seward (1712–1782), the first pastor of the Second Ecclesiastical Society of Killingworth. Henry Crane settled in the land granted to Killingworth. In 1704, the name of the settlement was changed to Durham. In 1708, Durham was incorporated as a town by the General Assembly. In the same year, the land previously granted to Killingworth was restored to Durham for the consideration of sixty acres in fee simple paid to Killingworth by Durham.

Settlers began moving into the northern part of Killingworth shortly after 1700. Those present in 1716 include Isaac Kelsey, Esq., Dea. Joseph Wilcox, Dea. Josiah Hull, Dea. Daniel Buell, John Wilcox, Joseph Griswold, Nathaniel Parmelee, Ebenezer Hull, Samuel Stevens, and Edward Rutty.

These were followed shortly by Solomon Davis, Timothy Chittenden, and Theophilus Redfield. Those residents living near the shore were merchants, tradesmen, fishermen, shipbuilders, and sailors, as well as farmers, while those in the north were almost exclusively farmers and referred to themselves as such. The northern residents became concerned because it was very difficult for them to regularly make the trip south to church and town meetings in a time when it was almost mandatory to attend. The northern settlers had to travel five to eight miles on foot, on horseback, or in wagons over poorly maintained muddy roads and the trip was especially difficult in winter. At some point, they decided there was a need to form their own parish or Second Ecclesiastical Society.

In 1734, the northern inhabitants petitioned the General Assembly to form a new society. On May 8, 1735, an Act of Organization was passed by the General Assembly. "Att a Generall Assembly Holden at Hartford May: 8 : 1[735] An act Dividing the Town of Killingworth in the Coun[ty] of New-london into two Distinct Ecclesiastical Societies." The act stated where the division line would be and made the northern part of town a separate ecclesiastical society. This line would be the boundary between Clinton and Killingworth. The new society is referred to in the records variously as the Second Ecclesiastical Society, North Society, North Parish, or North Killingworth. The ecclesiastical society held responsibility within its boundaries for religious affairs, schools, and the burying grounds. Property within the limit of a society was taxable, on vote of the society, for the support of the gospels and for the schools.

At the first meeting of the new society in 1735, it was decided to build a meetinghouse. On September 25, 1735 . "it twas voted that it twas necessary to Buld a meeting hous." A tax was set at a "Rate of a penc half pen[c] upon ye pound to defrae the Society Charges." The General Assembly appointed a committee to set the place for the meetinghouse. It reported on May 13, 1736, that they "have pitched upon a place upon a stony hill northerly from the new bridge over the Bare-Swamp brook, where we marked a walnut tree with the letter M, and laid some stones at the root of said staddle, which stands about forty or fifty rods from said bridge." The report was accepted and approved by the Assembly and "said society is ordered to proceed to build their meeting house upon the place pitched upon by said committee."

The building, however, became a society house or town hall instead of a meetinghouse as indicated by the following vote. "At a meeting of ye north Society in Killingworth . . . March : ye 25th : Day AD: 1736 : . . . it was voted that ye Society hous agreed to be bult Shall be Set up about eight or ten rods northeast from ye place afixed for ye Seting of ye meeting hous." The society house was 30 feet long and 22 feet wide. It was one story high and had a chimney at one end. This building was built in 1736, but probably because of delays in hiring a minister and establishing a church, and a "misunderstanding" concerning funds due the Second Society from the First Society for building a meetinghouse in the First Society, the building of a meetinghouse was delayed, and it was not until 1743 that the meetinghouse was completed. The society house was used for town and public meetings and stood for a considerable period of time. The site of the society house and meetinghouse is south of the Route 80 and 81 traffic circle and west of Route 81 on land owned by the Killingworth Land Conservation Trust.

The new society established its own church and chose a minister. A committee was formed to learn whether Mr. Samuel Eliot intended to enter the ministry. Samuel Eliot was the eldest son of Jared Eliot and graduated from Yale College in 1735. Sadly, he was in poor health and died at age 26 on a voyage to Africa taken to improve his health. It was then voted to hire Mr. William Seward to preach for several months and in 1737 he was called to be pastor. He was ordained on January 18, 1738 at the meetinghouse in the First Society. The General Assembly gave permission for the formation of a church on May 12, 1737. "Upon the memorial of the north society of Killingsworth: This Assembly grants liberty to the inhabitants of said society to imbody into church estate, with the approbation of their neighboring churches." Part of the agreement with Mr. Seward was that the Society would provide him with a house. A house 34 feet long and 28 feet wide was built. It was located at the present intersection of Routes 80 and 81. It burned after the Rev. Seward's death after which the existing center hall colonial house was built on the foundation. This house was used as the Killingworth Inn and then the Killingworth Café.

After obtaining a minister and establishing the church, the society resumed plans for building a meetinghouse. On November 5, 1739, "it twas voted that we will go about building a meeting house for the worship of God this year _ at the same meeting it was voted that wee will build s[d] house fifty Eight feet in Length & thurty Eight feet in bredth." This building was considerably larger than the society house. The meetinghouse was completed in 1743 and was used until 1820 when the second meetinghouse was completed and dedicated.

The Second Society also established its first burying ground, now the Union District Cemetery on Roast Meat Hill Road, on March 22, 1738. As the town grew, additional burying grounds were laid out throughout the town so that most of the school districts had their own cemetery.

Those living in the northern part of town wanted to have a school near their homes. The town voted at a town meeting on February 26, 1732/3: "Sundry of our northern farmers desireing liberty to sit up a School house on the hig way near wolf meadow was voated and granted." This is the first record of a schoolhouse in North Killingworth and it was probably located on Roast Meat Hill Road near the cemetery. School Districts were formed and often changed, combined with others, or new ones created. In the eighteenth century, the school districts were the Meetinghouse, Lane, Southwest Corner, Roastmeat Hill, Chesnut Hill, Tower Hill, Parmele, Parker Hill, Nettelton, Stone House, and Black Rock Districts. The Tower Hill, Roast Meat Hill, and Parmelee schools were consolidated into the Union District school in 1800. By the mid-nineteenth century, the town had eight school districts, each with its own one room schoolhouse. The districts were Center, Southwest, Chestnut Hill, Union, Lane, Pine Orchard, Stone House, and Black Rock. The one-room schoolhouses were used through 1948.

In 1816, the Second Ecclesiastical Society voted to build a new meetinghouse. The present Congregational Church building was raised in 1817 and completed in 1820. It was dedicated to the service of God on May 31, 1820. The design of the meetinghouse has traditionally been attributed to Ithiel Town, a well-known architect of the period from Connecticut.

The first meetinghouse was dismantled and rebuilt behind the new meetinghouse in 1822. It became the society house or town hall and stood until the 1880s. The next town hall was the Agricultural Hall built near the church in 1881. The present town hall on Route 81 was a house built in 1830 by Dr. Rufus Turner who purchased the property of Moses and Aaron Wilcox, twin brothers who moved from Killingworth and founded Twinsburg, Ohio.

Emmanuel Episcopal Church was organized in the late eighteenth century as the Episcopalian Society of North Bristol (now North Madison). The Society organized itself as a parish on July 10, 1800. Nineteen of the original members were from North Bristol and two were residents of North Killingworth. An influx of members from North Killingworth soon after changed the balance of the Society and it became known as the Episcopalian Society of North Bristol and North Killingworth. In 1802, the Society voted to construct a church in Killingworth on land belonging to Bezaleel Bristol "near Miss Lucy Blatchley's." Construction began in May of 1803 and a group of members from North Bristol decided they would build their own church in North Bristol. The church was never built and the members compromised in 1805 by naming the church in Killingworth the Union Church. Bezaleel Bristol quit-claimed the land to the church in 1807. The church was completed in 1816 and the sanctuary was consecrated by Bishop Hobart of New York in 1817. The first minister of the church was Nathan Bennett Burgess who had been rector of Christ Church in Guilford and St. John's in North Guilford. In 1869, Dr. Samuel Fuller, who served as priest in charge from 1867 to 1874, suggested the name be changed from Union Church to Emmanuel Church.

Present Killingworth did not become fully separated from Clinton as a Town until 1838. At that time, the two societies were nearly equal in population. The formation of the Second Ecclesiastical Society solved the problem of the northern farmers having a more convenient place of worship. However, they still had to travel south to attend town meetings. A compromise was reached whereby town meetings were held alternately in the southern and northern parts of town. This was probably not satisfactory to anyone and it became inevitable that the complete severance of North Killingworth from the southern section would have to take place. In addition, there were political differences. The northern section was strongly Democratic while the southern section was strongly Whig. The town also had a large debt, possibly for educational expenses or maintaining roads in the northern section. The northern residents favored a special tax to cover the debt while the southern residents opposed it. The southerners called for partition while the northerners opposed it. When the split occurred by an act of the Legislature in May, 1838, it was highly favorable to North Killingworth which retained the name Killingworth, the original town records, rights to the town dock and beach, and two representatives to the General Assembly.

The principal occupation in Killingworth was farming, and from the founding of the town the residents were known as "the farmers." The town, however, grew considerably and contained many small industries. In 1814, the grand list for North Killingworth was $31,645.65, with 212 dwelling houses and three merchant stores. The industries included saw mills, grist mills, shingle mills, flour mills, paper mills, carding mills, feed mills, fulling mills, axe helve or axe handle manufactories, tanneries, blacksmith's shop, doctor's office, store, tavern, and meat market. In 1874, L. E. Stevens was a "Dealer in Dry Goods, Groceries, Yankee Notions, &c., and in fact, all Goods kept in a well conducted Country store." The Redfield store, later the first Killingworth Inn, was located north of the Ely house on Route 81. There were two iron mills or forges, one on Ironworks Road on the Menunketesuck River and the other in Chatfield Hollow. These forges first made iron from bog iron found in the bogs and swamps. The forge off Ironworks Road was operated by Jared Eliot and his son Dr. Aaron Eliot. A paper mill was located on Paper Mill Road. In 1835, Abner Lane, an inventor and scientist, founded the A. Lane & Co., Makers of Axe and Pick Axe Handles, which operated two axe handle factories.

With the opening of the Erie Canal and then the railroads, agricultural products from the Midwest were able to reach eastern markets. Throughout New England, the farms with their mostly rocky soils were unable to compete with the lower cost products from the Midwest, and local farmers sold their land and moved to the Midwest. The population in Killingworth declined from 1,130 at the time of the split with Clinton to 528 in 1890 to 482 in 1932. The grand list decreased from $306,702 in 1858 to $225,004 in 1883. Around the turn of the century, immigrants from European countries began to move into town. They bought the farms of the descendants of the original settlers at very low prices. Most continued to farm and operate dairy and chicken farms, mostly at a subsistence level. This influx of new people was responsible for many of the early homesteads being preserved. Those houses that were not purchased were abandoned and fell into ruin, as did all of the mills.

In the first half of the twentieth century, Killingworth was an isolated rural community and was among the last to receive telephone, paved roads, and electricity. Schools were held in one-room schoolhouses until 1948. Population began to increase in the 1950s as people began moving from the cities to the suburbs, aided by the construction of the Connecticut Turnpike. Killingworth was attractive because of its relatively rural atmosphere and fine school system. Population continued to increase greatly with new residential development but has slowed in recent years. Today, Killingworth is primarily a residential community.

Gravestones

The imagery on the earliest gravestones in America is derived from the strong and stern religious beliefs of the Puritans. Except for gravestones, the Puritans avoided all forms of religious symbols as a form of idolatry. Gravestones may have been the exception because the church did not exert authority over the burying grounds, but passed them into civic hands. Except for private cemeteries that were established later, the authority over the original graveyards still remains with the towns, which bear the responsibility for their care. Initially, the dominant themes on gravestones were mortality and preparedness for death as expressed, for example, in the winged death's head. Around the middle of the eighteenth century, the motifs on gravestones began to emphasize resurrection and life-everlasting and the winged soul effigy replaced the death's head. This change coincided with the revivalist Great Awakening that began around 1740. The New England iconography began to disappear by the beginning of the nineteenth century, replaced by the neoclassical willows and urns, and vanished in the twentieth century. Throughout their history, gravestones have reflected the current popular piety and religious sentiments of the time.

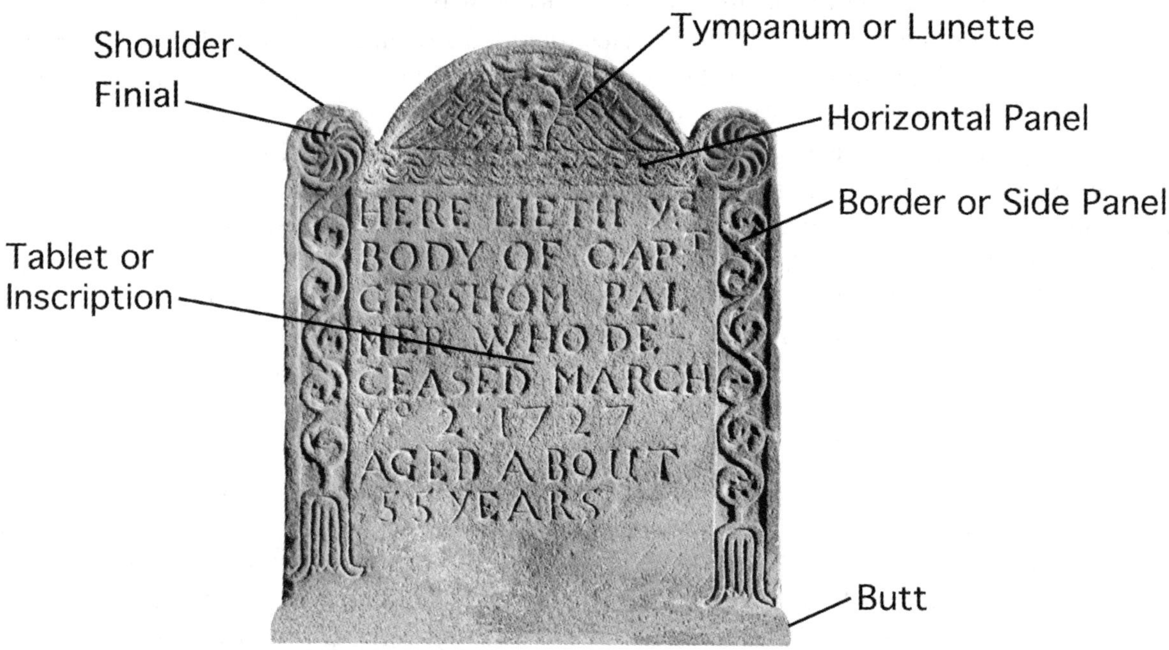

Parts of a gravestone.

The materials used in making most of the gravestones in Killingworth were gneiss, sandstone, and marble. There are a small number of slate stones in the Indian River Cemetery. The great majority of fieldstones and light grey rock gravestones of the mid-eighteenth century in Killingworth are composed of gneiss. This is not surprising since Killingworth is almost entirely underlain by Monson gneiss that forms a mass known as the Killingworth Dome. Gneiss is a foliated metamorphic rock in which the coarse mineral grains have been arranged into a banded structure. The light colored bands are composed mostly of quartz and feldspars and the dark bands contain a high percentage of biotite, a black mica. Some of the gneiss gravestones have granitic veins. Sandstone was the predominant material of the eighteenth century. Sandstone is a sedimentary rock composed mainly of quartz and feldspar grains. It allows for low relief sculpture. Most of the gravestones are brown sandstones from the quarries in the Chatham (Portland) area. Unfortunately, this sandstone is subject to interior disintegration with blistering and scaling of the face of the gravestone. Many of the sandstone gravestones in Killingworth cemeteries have been lost and others are deteriorating rapidly. A more durable red sandstone came from the Windsor area. There was also a quarry in Middlefield that was the source of some sandstone. Sandstone was replaced by white marble in the nineteenth century. Marble is a metamorphosed limestone. It is relatively soft and can be carved in sculpted relief but is not very durable. Granite, usually with a polished surface, appeared at the end of the nineteenth century. Granite has the same composition as gneiss but is an igneous rock with randomly arranged grains.

Sandstone gravestone in which the face has sloughed off.
Union District Cemetery.

At first, stones gathered from the field were used as grave markers. These were followed by gneiss stones with initials, dates, or names carved into them. The earliest local carvers are unknown. They were not professional gravestone carvers but could have been a stonemason, bricklayer, slater, cordwainer, carpenter, or blacksmith. Some stones were most likely made by friends or neighbors of the deceased, perhaps on short notice. The Rev. William C. Knowles, priest at Emmanuel Episcopal Church in the late nineteenth century, carved boulders for families too poor to erect a monument.

Professional carvers existed since the late seventeenth century. Some of those working in the Connecticut Valley have been identified. Although no study of Killingworth stones has been done, the presence of stones of the same style in other towns whose carvers are known allows the makers of some Killingworth gravestones to be identified.

Three generations of the Johnson family produced gravestones found throughout the lower Connecticut Valley. They worked out of the brown sandstone quarries in Portland. Thomas Johnson I (1690–1761) produced the winged skull stones with hollow eyes, triangular nose, and row of teeth. Several of these stones are present in the Indian River Cemetery and Old Durham Cemetery. It is likely some stones in Killingworth were carved by his son Thomas II and grandson Thomas III.

Winged death's head, Isaac Griswold stone, 1727. Indian River Cemetery, Thomas Johnson I carver.

Three carvers who worked in the area between about 1750 and 1770 were William Holland, David Miller, and Ichabod Higgins. They produced soul effigies with round or oval faces and down-swept wings. The numeral one on the stones is in the shape of a "J". William Holland worked out of Middletown. David Miller (1718–1789) was a Middlefield carver and owned a quarry in that town. Ichabod Higgins (1738–1773) is buried in the Old Durham Cemetery. Their gravestones are very similar in style and it is likely the carvers were closely associated and may have worked together.

Winged soul effigies of the Holland/Miller/Higgins types on Concurrence Seaward stone, 1753, and Mabel Seward stone, 1769. Union District Cemetery.

The majority of markers in Killingworth from the latter part of the eighteenth century were made by John Johnson (1748–1826). He lived in Haddam and Durham and is not known to be related to the other Johnson carvers. There are two styles of his gravestones. In one, the wings of the soul effigy curve downward like heavy ear lobes and in the other they sweep up from below the face and end in sharp points. The latter stones have more carving and details than the former. The border panels on his stones are elaborate scroll and drapery designs. The latest gravestone by Johnson is the 1816 Zerviah Kelsey stone in the Union District Cemetery.

Two styles of soul effigies by John Johnson; Charles Lord stone, 1790, and Daniel Buell stone, 1782. Union District Cemetery.

John Johnson and his wife, Abigail, bought the c1750 house at 19 Maiden Lane in Durham in 1773. Maiden Lane is named after five unmarried daughters. It is said they went everywhere together in single file in order of their ages. They lived into old age and, when the last one died, her gravestone read "The Last One."

Nabby Hurd, 1795. Indian River Cemetery.

Finally, there are some late eighteenth and early nineteenth century gravestones like the Nabby Hurd stone that have an unusual form of the effigy with wide down-curved wings swirling upward in a rams-horn shape. This is referred to as the flared ear style (Slater, 1987). Some gravestones in the flared ear style were carved by Charles Dolph.

The Gravestone Styles of the Killingworth Area

The styles of gravestones and their evolution in the Killingworth area are described in this chapter. There are very few seventeenth century markers in the area and possibly only a few hundred in New England. Many undoubtedly have been lost but the major reason for the scarcity of stones is that in the early days of settlement people were buried in unmarked graves. Wooden markers were used but these have disappeared. The earliest grave markers were plain fieldstones as they were readily available and there were no stone carvers in the area. There are a large number of plain fieldstone markers in the Killingworth cemeteries. The 1934 survey lists over 150 fieldstones in the Union District Cemetery and over 100 in the Pine Orchard District Cemetery. There are not as many fieldstones visible today, but many are probably buried. Fieldstones continued to be used after carvers were available and it is likely many of these are the markers of those unable to afford a carved gravestone. As expected for fieldstones, they appear in a variety of shapes but many seem to have been selected to resemble a marker and some may have been crudely shaped. There are some examples, especially in the Union District Cemetery, where the headstone is accompanied by a smaller fieldstone footstone.

Fieldstone markers. Union District Cemetery.

Fieldstone headstones and footstones. Union District Cemetery.

The earliest dated markers are upright rectangular gneiss stones in the Indian River Cemetery (the Killingworth Yard). They bear initials and a date, as on the DK 1676 stone in the Kelsey plot. A similar but later gravestone, AW 1742, probably a Wilcox, stands in the Union District Cemetery.

"DK 1676 12 March." Indian River Cemetery. An infant son of Daniel and Mary Kelsey.

"1742 AW DieD March 28." Union District Cemetery. 9"w x 19"h.

" TP." Red sandstone.

"1745 JP." Josiah Parmelee, Jr., d April 10, 1745.

Union District Cemetery.

Other early markers are simple gneiss or sandstone stones. These markers can be plain with no lettering, but can have initials as on the TP stone or initials and a date as on the JP stone. These initialed stones probably belong to members of the Parmelee family. They can have a name as on the Siah Buell stone or a name and date as on the Mercy Parmele marker. Some have a more complete inscription as on the Buell infant stone. Some have rounded tops and clearly been shaped. These simple markers lack symbols of any kind.

"1744 Mercy Parmele."

Plain, shaped marker. Union District Cemetery.

"Siah Buell."

Gneiss marker for an infant son of Aaron & Hannah Buell, 1758. Union District Cemetery.

Tripartite stone. Thankful Johnson, 1738. Old Durham Cemetery.

Although symbols were used on gravestones in Boston and other metropolitan areas along the coast much earlier, they began to appear in this area around 1725. Their use became more extensive and evolved as the century progressed. The types of symbols and their associations form an identifiable pattern that has been termed the Connecticut Valley ornamental style (Ludwig, 1966).

Most of the gravestones are tripartite in shape with a large central arch flanked by two smaller ones. The Thankful Johnson stone is an early example of the tripartite marker which is the predominant form of gravestone in the eighteenth century. This shape represents a door or portal through which the soul of the deceased passes from the mortal world on the way to eternal life. Some of the first tripartite stones have no symbols and others have a few simple designs. However, the predominant symbol in the first quarter of the eighteenth century is the winged death's head.

The James Hickox stone in the Old Durham Yard shows some of the first symbols in the form of pinwheels on the finials. Most of the death's head markers in the area were made by Thomas Johnson I. They consist of a menacing-looking skull with wings. The border panels are continuous scrolls or fig-like designs and there is a double scroll beneath the skull. An example of this style is seen in the Isaac Griswould stone. Stones with the death's head are in the Indian River and Durham Cemeteries but there are none in Killingworth.

Around 1740, the death's head began a transition into the winged soul effigy. The death's head loses its lower jaw although the teeth may persist as serrations on the bottom of the jaw as in the Samuel Bates stone. A vestigial jaw is present on the Josiah Kelcey and Isaac Kelcey Esq. stones. The skull is transformed into a round or oval expressionless face as on the Theophilus Redfield gravestone. The hollow eyes and triangular nose are lost. The decorations are relatively simple and consist of vines on the borders.

James Hickox, 1725. Old Durham Cemetery.

Isaac Griswould, 1727. Indian River Cemetery.

Samuel Bates, 1750. Old Durham Cemetery.

Josiah Kelcey, 1758. Indian River Cemetery.

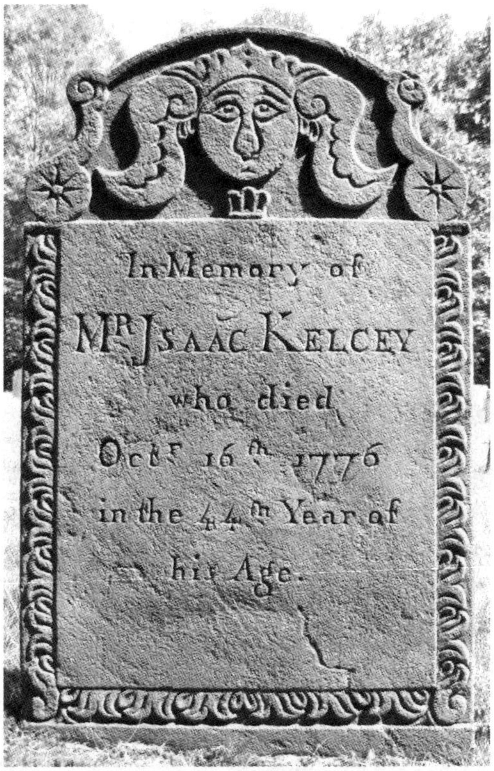

Isaac Kelcey Esq., 1751. Southwest District Cemetery.

Theophilus Redfield, 1759. Southwest District Cemetery.

Samuel Steevens, 1760. Union District Cemetery.

Sarah Griswold, 1784. Union District Cemetery.

The theme most used by rural carvers in the second half of the eighteenth century was that of the flight of the soul to heaven illustrated by the winged soul effigy. This reflected a change in Puritan thought from mortality and death to an emphasis on resurrection and immortality. This change coincided with the Great Awakening which began around 1740 led by George Whitefield and Jonathan Edwards. Whereas under Puritanism, only a select few were elected for salvation, the revivalist movement taught that all men can be saved. The Isaac Kelcey Esq. stone has a winged face that retains elements of the skull in the sunken eyes and elongated chin. The Theophilus Redfield stone has nearly completed the transition to the soul effigy but the general design of the face is still reminiscent of the skull. Many of the stones are relatively plain with a winged soul effigy with a crown as seen in the Samuel Steevens stone.

Jerusha Parmele, 1786. Union District Cemetery.

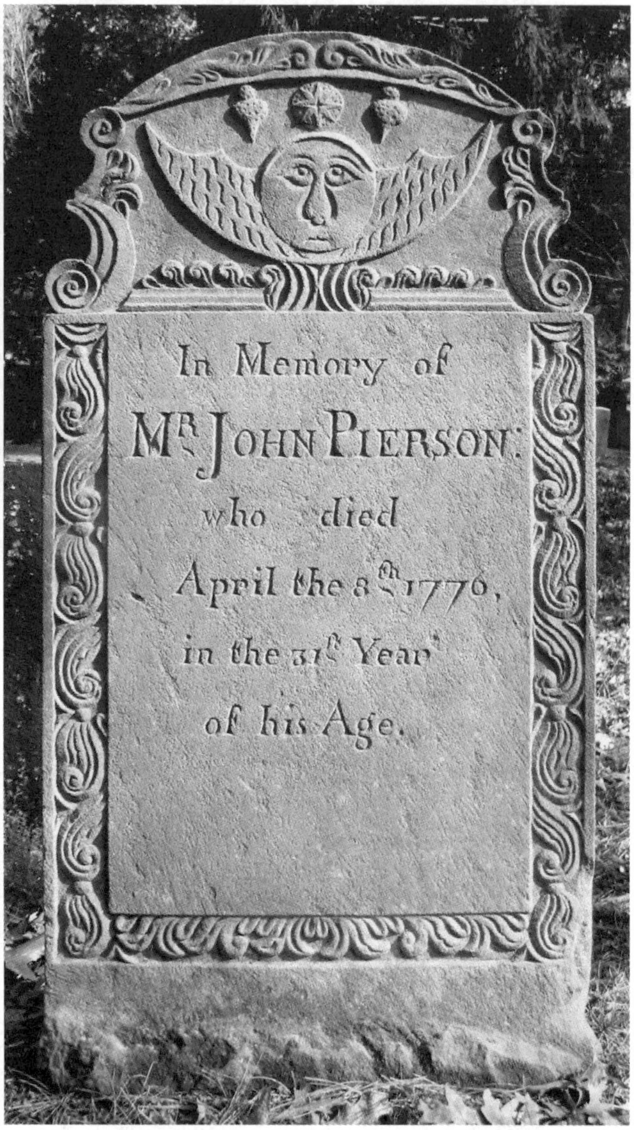

John Pierson, 1776. Union District Cemetery.

The gravestones most characteristic of Killingworth are those by John Johnson in the latter part of the eighteenth century. The face of the soul effigy is round and most bear a crown. The wings sweep down and curl outward at the end. In the simpler stones, such as the Sarah Griswold stone, the designs are incised into the stone. In others, like the Mrs. Jerusha Parmele stone, the soul effigy and designs are in relief. The border panels have various scroll or drapery designs. Some of the stones are marked by more florid carving and the use of scroll motifs as seen in the John Pierson stone. The complexity of the design in these gravestones was probably reflected in the price. There are many of these stones in the Union and Southwest District Cemeteries. Flared ear style gravestones such as the Rachael Redfield stone appeared toward the end of the eighteenth century. These are most numerous in the Indian River Cemetery.

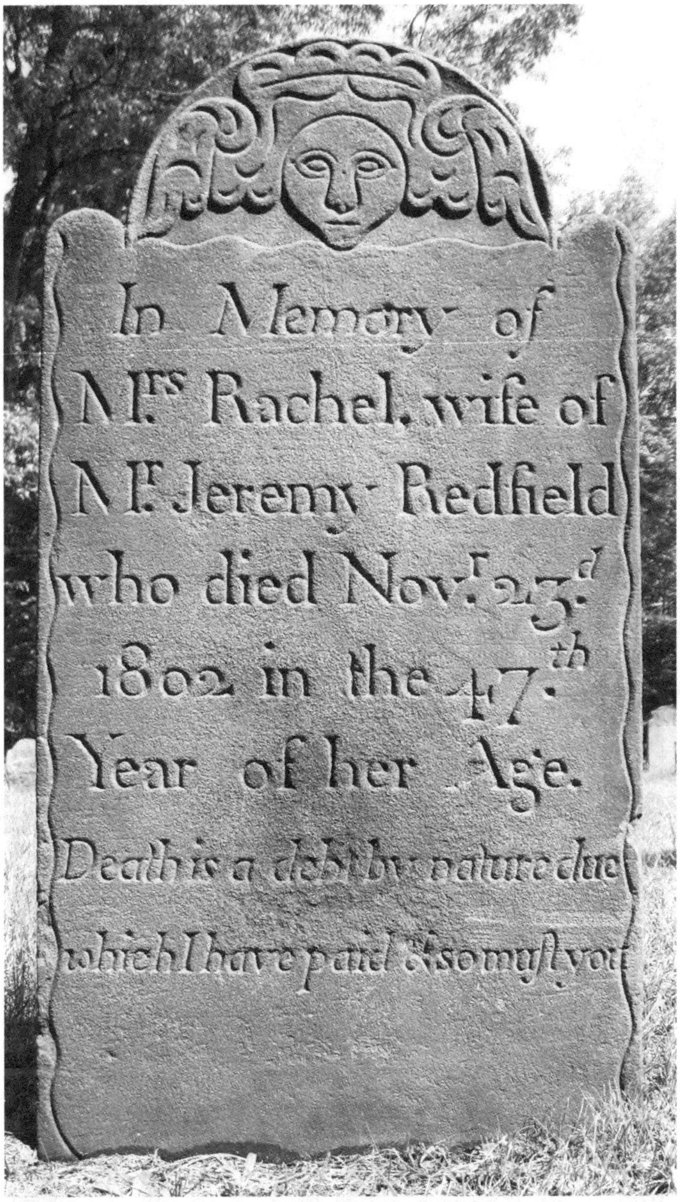

Rachel Redfield. 1802. Southwest District Cemetery.

Frederick Wilcox, 1819. Southwest District Cemetery.

Around 1800, the gravestones underwent a change from the Puritan religious spirit to an enthusiasm for classical antiquity. Neoclassical symbols such and urns and willows, as in the Frederick Wilcox and Martin Lord Esq. stones, became very popular. There are also many allegorical subjects such as pointing fingers (Ella Parmelee marker), clasped hands, drapery (Dorinda Harris stone), bibles, and doves. The inscriptions on some stones were in flowery script such as seen on the Concurrence Lord gravestone. There was expression of sentimentality through epitaphs and symbols like flowers and lambs.

Most of these markers are made of white marble, which is of great beauty when new. Unfortunately, it is not very durable and is susceptible to an unsightly black lichen that is extremely difficult to remove. There are a few transitional markers, such as the Frederick Wilcox stone, made of sandstone and tripartite in shape but bearing a neoclassical symbol. The marble neoclassical markers completely replaced the earlier form in a short period of time at the beginning of the nineteenth century.

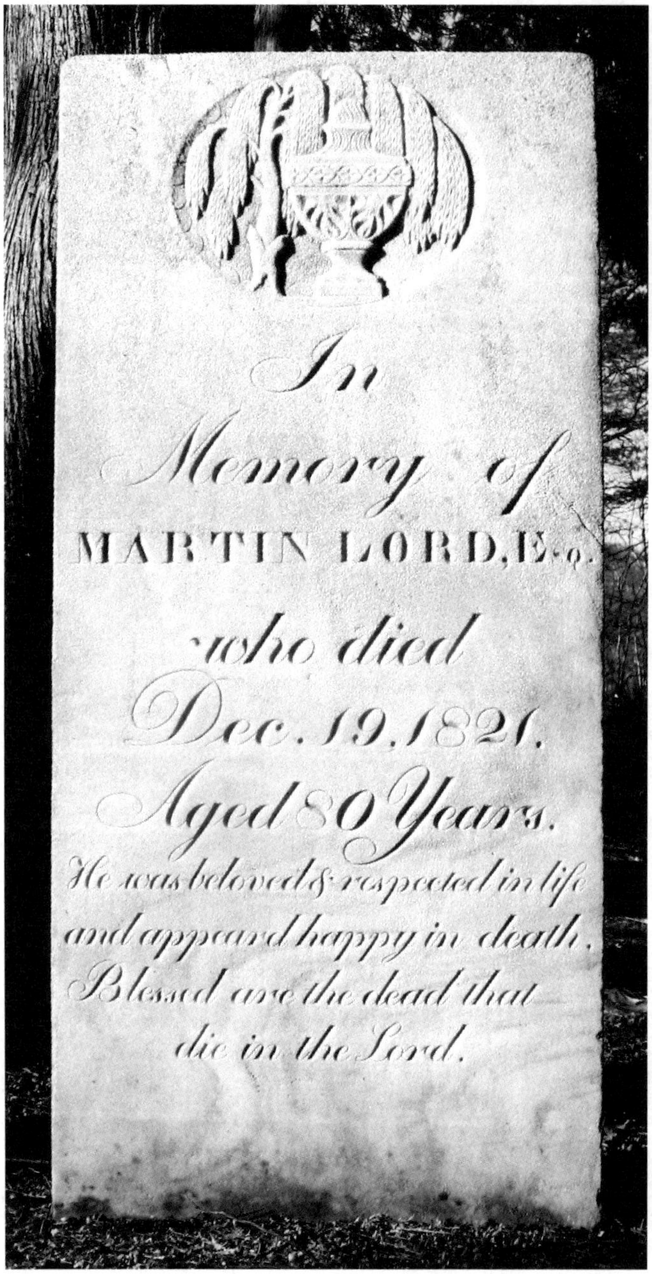

Martin Lord, Esq., 1821. Union District Cemetery.

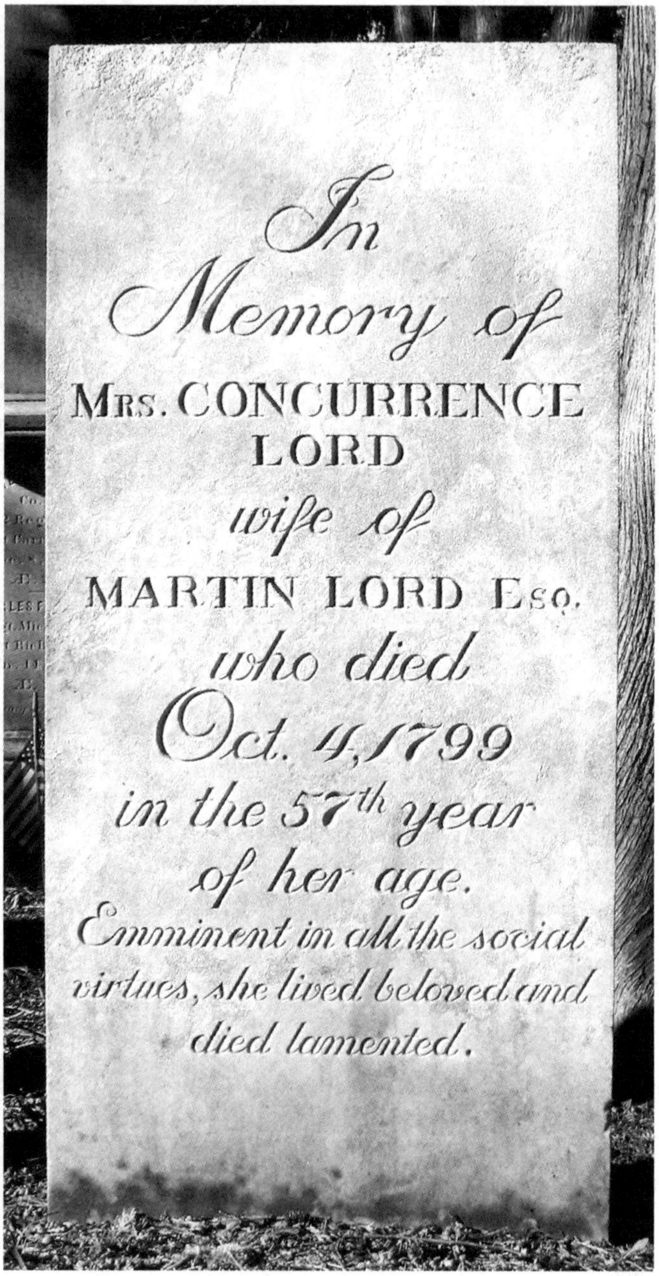

Concurrence Lord, 1799. Union District Cemetery.

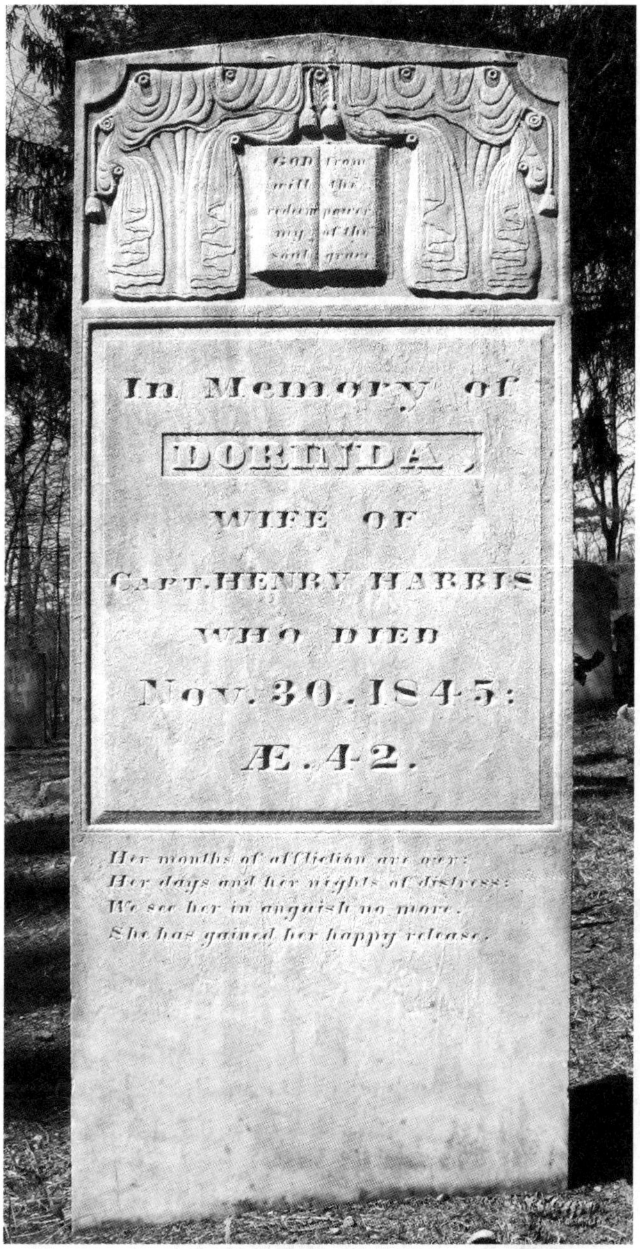

Dorinda Harris, 1845. Union District Cemetery.

Ella Parmelee, 1876. Evergreen Cemetery.

Although many markers have neoclassical symbols, the majority of the nineteenth century marble gravestones in Killingworth are relatively simple and plain. They have an inverted V top as on the Josephine Kelsey marker, a flat top as on the Martha Pratt stone, or a rounded top. These stones can have an epitaph but do not have symbols.

Different forms of gravestones began to appear toward the end of the nineteenth century. A few Latin crosses are seen. The cross for Jay Wallace bears a lily. The Grace Eliot Rogers monument is a Celtic cross that is actually pagan in origin but was adopted by Christianity. Some monuments such as the Johnny Lyne stone are in the form of a broken column that signifies early death or a life cut short.

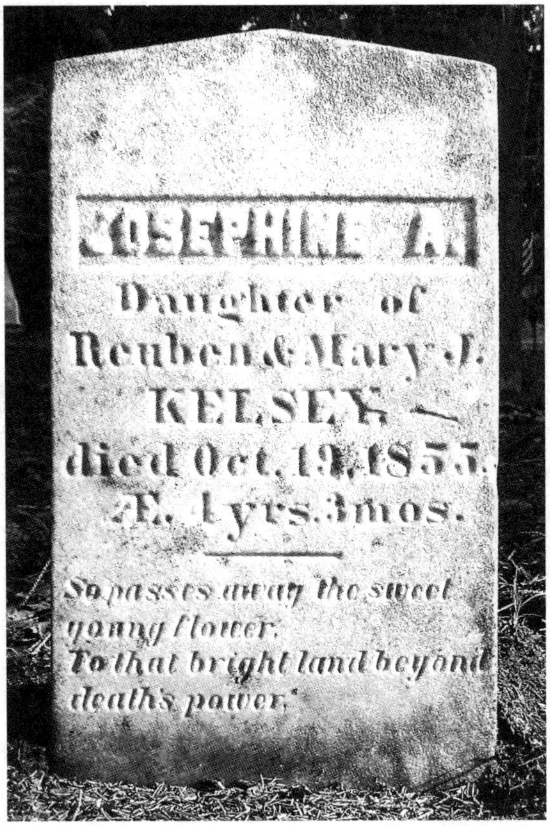

Josephine Kelsey, 1855. Union District Cemetery.

Martha Pratt, 1853. Union District Cemetery.

Jay Wallace, 1890.

Grace Eliot Rogers, 1934.
Indian River Cemetery.

Jonny Lyne, 1873.

At the end of the nineteenth century, large monuments, usually of granite, began to appear. These could be for individuals but were often for families, for example, the Wilcox and Turner granite monuments. Family monuments are often accompanied by small markers placed in front of or around the monument with the initials or first names of family members.

Wilcox and Turner Family monuments. Granite, Evergreen Cemetery.

A distinctive type of metal monument appeared at the end of the nineteenth century. They are easily recognized by their light blue color. The base is often cast to resemble stone as on the Julia Burrows monument. These monuments were made by the Monumental Bronze Company in Bridgeport, Connecticut between 1874 and 1914. They were called "white bronze" monuments but are actually made of zinc. On exposure to air, the monuments develop a coating of zinc carbonate that is responsible for the blue color. There were a large variety of sizes and shapes that could be viewed in catalogs and ordered through sales agents.

A few large, tall monuments also appeared. The Hull family monument is a sandstone obelisk with drapery on top.

Julia G. Burrows, 1907. Zinc monument, Indian River Cemetery.

Henry Hull Family monument. Evergreen Cemetery.

There are a small number of table tombs in the area such as the Theophilus Morgan tomb. These consist of a flat stone tablet supported by columns or pillars. Chest tombs are completely enclosed. The inscription occurs on the tablet. The body is buried under these tombs. Although not numerous, they were used over a period of 250 years.

Theophilus Morgan table tomb, 1788. Indian River Cemetery.

Samuel Redfield chest tomb, 1800. Indian River Cemetery.

Inscriptions

The inscription contains basic biographical data on the individual. The earliest in the area have only initials and a date. Typically, the inscription includes the name of the person, date of death, and age of the deceased. In the first part of the eighteenth century, the inscription often began with the somber words "Here lieth y^e^ body of." Later, this focus on mortality changed to the gentler "In Memory of."

Steven Hickcoox inscription showing misspelling of "here," a correction in which the stone was chiseled out, and use of u for a v. Old Durham Cemetery, 1725.

Inscription on Mary Lord stone showing a long S and use of titles. Union District Cemetery, 1790.

Most inscriptions are in block letters. On some nineteenth century marble stones like that of Dan Lane, a cursive script is used. Many of the early gravestones use old English lettering such as a long S (ʃ) for S at the beginning and middle of a word, or exchanged U and V and I and J. On some stones, two numbers are given for a year, for example, 1706/7. The first number is the year according to the older Julian calendar where the first day is March 25. The second number is the year according to the Gregorian calendar in which the first day of the new year is January 1. Catholic countries adopted the Gregorian calendar beginning in 1582 but England and the colonies did not until 1752. A few stones such as that of Concurrence Seaward have OS (Old Style) and NS (New Style) before or after the date to identify which system is used. Æ or Æt is often seen before the age of the person. This is an abbreviation for the Latin *Ætatis* meaning "aged." AD refers to *Anno Domini*, "in the year of the Lord."

Concurrence Seaward, 1753. Union District Cemetery.

"1742 John Steevens died October ye 9." Red sandstone, 10"w x 10"h, prominent guidelines, "ye" (lower right) inserted as a superscript. This stone was completely buried. Union District Cemetery.

Guidelines are sometimes used in early stones as seen on the John Steevens stone. Often, the lines were not straight. In some cases, a letter was left out and added as a superscript. If a carver ran out of space on a line, the word was continued on the next line. Mistakes in spelling were made. Sometimes, these were corrected by chiseling out the misspelled word, and carving the correct word in the depression.

Titles are often given before or after the names such as Mr, Ens, Lieut, Capt, Revd, Esq, and Dr. Esq or Esqr was used if the person was a justice, magistrate, judge, or connected to the legal profession. In the case of women, Miss or Mrs was used. If she was married, she was referred to as the wife, widow, consort (died before the husband), or relic or relict (archaic term for widow) of the husband. For children, the inscription usually denotes son or daughter and gives the names of the parents.

Dan Lane Esq., 1826, marble, 23 ½"w x 45 ½"h. Block and cursive lettering, Died AEt. 63.
Union District Cemetery.

Symbols

Symbols on gravestones have abstract meanings usually pertaining to the religious beliefs of the time. The earliest symbols reflect Puritan religious thought regarding life, death, resurrection, and eternal life. For an agrarian and largely illiterate society, the gravestone was an educational device and a pictorial representation of the religious philosophies of the day. While many people could not read the inscription on the gravestone, all, including the children, could recognize the symbols. Although most symbols in colonial New England have a Christian connotation, many originated in antiquity and were adopted by Christianity. The gravestones in Killingworth are rich in symbolism.

Winged Death's Head. One of the earliest symbols to appear on gravestones in the Killingworth area is the winged death's head. This symbol reflects the Puritan belief that one must pass through death to achieve eternal life. The skull represents mortality and the certainty of physical death. The wings, though, reflect the possibility of resurrection and transition to a new life. In addition, some of the skulls are crowned, signifying victory over death. Most of the skulls on gravestones in the area have sunken eyes, a triangular nose, and a row of teeth as on the Deacon Thomas Lyman stone. The Joseph Hickox stone bears an ominous skull. A crown is present on the skull of the Mary Eliot stone.

Deacon Thomas Lyman, 1725. Old Durham Cemetery.

Joseph Hickox, 1725. Old Durham Cemetery.

Mary Eliot, 1729. Indian River Cemetery.

Transitional Forms. There are a number of transitional forms between the winged death's head and the later winged soul effigy. The outline of the face in the Josiah Buell gravestone is that of a skull but the mouth lacks teeth. This is an unusual slate stone for the area and was probably made in Rhode Island. In the Samuel Bates stone, the lower jaw of the skull is lost but a row of serrated teeth remain. The face in the Abiel Pierson stone is very similar to the Bates face, but wears a small crown. The skull in the Abigail Wadsworth stone also has the row of serrated teeth but wears a larger crown and larger downswept wings. The winged face on the Bathsheba Griswould stone resembles a skull without teeth. On stones such as the John Grant stone, the face is intermediate between a skull and soul effigy. On the John Seaward stone, the thin elongated lower jaw, empty eye sockets, abstract nose, and slash for a mouth are carryovers from the death's head symbolism. On the Josiah Kelsey and Isaac Kelcey Esq. stones, the elongated jaw is all that remains of the skull image.

Josiah Buell, 1732. Slate, Indian River Cemetery.

Samuel Bates, 1750. Old Durham Cemetery.

Abiel Peirson, 1751. Indian River Cemetery.

Abigail Wadsworth, 1748/9. Old Durham Cemetery.

Bathsheba Griswould. 1737. Indian River Cemetery.

John Grant, 1736. Old Durham Cemetery.

John Seaward 1st, 1750. Union District Cemetery.

Josiah Kelcey, 1758. Indian River Cemetery.

Isaac Kelcey Esq., 1751. Southwest District Cemetery.

Winged Soul Effigy. The winged soul effigy consists of a face representing the soul of the deceased. The face is flanked by wings that will carry the soul to heaven. The first soul effigies that completed the transition from the death's head appeared in Killingworth around 1750. In the Martha Buell stone, the face is that of a cherub, another symbol for the soul of the deceased. This is another slate stone uncommon in the area and was probably made in Rhode Island. The Capt. John Lane stone has a plain face and wings. The unusual effigy on the Hannah Lane stone also has a plain face but the head arises from a neck and appears to have downswept hair. Although this may be a simple form of the winged soul effigy, it could also be a portrait effigy in which the face is that of Hannah. Winged soul effigies with crowns are seen on the Capt. Josiah Hull, Aaron Nettelton, and Elisabeth Hull stones. Around 1770, the sandstone gravestones by John Johnson began appearing and are the most numerous late eighteenth century markers in North Killingworth. The soul effigy has a nearly round face, eyes with pupils, bulbous nose, small mouth, and a crown. The wings sweep straight down and curl up at the ends. The effigy could be carved into the stone as on the Benjamin Lord stone or in relief as on the Lemuel Hull stone.

Martha Buell, 1740. Indian River Cemetery.

Capt. John Lane, 1755. Union District Cemetery.

Hannah Lane, 1744. Indian River Cemetery.

Capt. Josiah Hull, 1753. Union District Cemetery.

Aaron Nettelton, 1759. Southwest District Cemetery.

Elisabeth Hull, 1769. Southwest District Cemetery.

Benjamin Lord, 1786. Union District Cemetery.

Lemuel Hull, 1793. Southwest District Cemetery.

Toward the end of the eighteenth century, some gravestones in the area began to show the influence of the baroque style, a style that was fluid and elaborate with many details and ornaments. It was popular in the urban coastal areas while in rural areas it influenced but did not replace the traditional style of stones. This change can be seen in the second type of John Johnson's gravestones. In the John Seward and John Pierson stones, the face of the soul effigy is unchanged. However, the wings are upswept and end in points. The soul effigy is now surrounded by scrolls and various symbols. These gravestones which were undoubtedly more expensive than Johnson's simpler style and were generally used for prominent persons.

John P. Seward, 1784. Union District Cemetery.

John Pierson, 1776. Union District Cemetery.

A second distinctive type of gravestone showing a baroque influence appears in Killingworth at the end of the eighteenth century. These stones have a distinctive form termed the "flared ear style"

(Slater, 1987). They have a ram's horn swirl within the wings. The face has a chin and the eyes are well-defined. The face is usually flat as in the Esther Lord stone or in rounded relief as on the Eliphaz Willcox stone. There is a large crown continuous with the wings. The William Lord stone has the same face as the others but the wings are small and upswept and the crown is separate. These stones are fine-grained, dark red sandstone that is very durable. The late eighteenth century gravestones represent the final phase of the Connecticut Valley ornamental style. It was abruptly replaced around 1800 by the neoclassical style that employed entirely new symbols.

Esther Lord, 1799. Union District Cemetery.

Eliphaz Willcox, 1803. Southwest District Cemetery.

William Lord, 1799. Union District Cemetery.

Rosette, Pinwheel, Coil. Rosettes, pinwheels, coils, whorls and similar symbols were among the first to appear on Killingworth gravestones often occurring in the finials. The six-pointed rosette, as seen on the Josiah Kelcey stone, is an ancient symbol. It was common on Hellenistic provincial gravestones and was brought to England by the Romans. The design may represent the petals of a rose or flower. The pinwheel, as seen on the Capt. Gershom Palmer stone, suggests the cosmic motion of the heavens. The concentric geometric coil or whorl as on the Abigail Pierson stone probably has a similar meaning.

Josiah Kelsey, 1758.

Capt. Gershom Palmer, 1727.
Indian River Cemetery.

Abigail Pierson, 1727.

Vine. In Christian tradition, the churches are considered to be the vineyards and the congregations are the vines. Many of the eighteenth century gravestones in Killingworth have continuous foliate and floral ornamental border panels. Vines with different patterns of leaves are present on the Josiah Kelcey, John Seaward, Eunice Bristol, Elisabeth Hull, and Nathan Kelcey stones. The leaves on the Eunice Bristol stone appear to be acanthus leaves, one of the oldest cemetery motifs originating in ancient Greece. On the Leut. Samuell Parsons stone, a flower arises from the vine and fills the finial. The Bathsheba Griswould vine has leaves and flowers. On the Henry Crane and Mabel Seaward stones, flowers occur along the length of the vine. Ivy, as occurs on the polished granite Wright Family monument, is a symbol of fidelity and immortality because it is eternally green. Because it clings to a support, it also symbolizes attachment, affection, and friendship.

Patterns of vines on border panels. Josiah Kelcey, 1758, Indian River; John Seaward 2nd, 1763, Union District; Eunice Bristol, 1755, Pine Orchard; Elisabeth Hull, 1769, Southwest District; Capt. Nathan Kelcey, 1751, Southwest District Cemetery.

Ivy, Wright Family monument, 1937. Indian River Cemetery.

Vines with flowers. Leut. Samuell Parsons, 1734, Old Durham; Bathsheba Griswould, 1737, Indian River; Dea. Henry Crane, 1741, Old Durham; Mabel Seaward, 1768, Union District Cemetery.

Crown. The crown of righteousness appears on many of the eighteenth century gravestones. It represents the triumph over death and the glory of the victorious soul arisen to heaven through Christ. A crown occupies the entire lunette of the John Seward stone. In the Nathan Hull stone, the soul effigy wears a crown and there is another underneath.

John Seward, 1748. Old Durham Cemetery.

Nathan Hull, 1813. Union District Cemetery.

Star. Stars are a symbol of the heavens. A single star often signifies the Star of the East that guided the Magi to Bethlehem. A star occurs at the top of the Deacon Dodo Pierson and Heil Hull gravestones.

Deacon Dodo Pierson, 1796. Union District Cemetery.

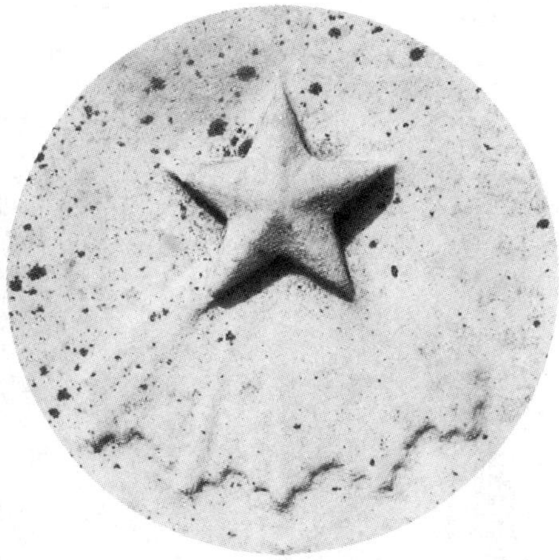

Heil Hull, 1867. Indian River Cemetery.

Hourglass and Sundial. The hourglass and sundial signify the passage of time. They, like the winged death's head, are *memento mori*, reminders of mortalty and death. The lunette of the Elisabeth Steevens stone is occupied by an hourglass and the words "TEMPUS FUGIT." The sundail sits on top of the Jean Nicolas monument, and bears the message LIGHT FOLLOWS DARKNESS.

Elisabeth Steevens, 1748.

Dr. Jean Henri Nicolas, 1937.

Indian River Cemetery.

Urn. The urn was the first neoclassical symbol to appear in Killingworth cemeteries. They occur first on tripartite gravestones and then on the later flat-topped stones like that of Hezekiah Lane. The urn on the Hannah Gale gravestone is an especially fine carving on slate. The draped urn on the Elizabeth Farnham stone is an unusual high relief carving in sandstone. Although many of these neoclassical symbols are derived from those in ancient Greece, they have taken on strong Christian religious meanings. The urn was a Greek symbol of mourning. On gravestones, the urn represents the body as a container of the soul and is a symbol of immortality. The urn is also a repository for the ashes of the deceased and a symbol of death of the flesh, but cremations were seldom performed at the time they appeared. Urns may be draped signifying mourning or representing the veil between the earth and the heavens. They may have a flame at the top indicating the eternal spirit of man or eternal life.

Hezekiah Lane, 1809. Sandstone, Union District Cemetery.

Hannah Gale, 1797. Slate, Indian River Cemetery.

Elizabeth Farnham, 1814. Indian River.

Willow and Urn. The willow and urn commonly occur together as on the Jonathan Kelsey and Martin Lord stones. Both are Greek Revival symbols of mourning. The weeping willow signifies sadness and mourning with the long draping strands suggesting the hair of a woman bent over in grief. It also indicates that man, like a tree, must reach for heaven and the joy of celestial life. The urn contains the remains of the deceased and represents death but is also the container from which the soul arises to heaven.

Jonathan Kelsey, 1835. Lane District Cemetery.

Martin Lord Esq., 1821. Union District Cemetery.

Tapestry. Tapestries or draperies signify mortality and mourning. The draperies on the Dorinda Harris stone are parted to reveal a book with the inscription "God will redeem my soul from the power of the grave." The opening in the draperies symbolizes the passage through which the soul will travel.

Dorinda Harris, 1845. Union District Cemetery.

Anna Griswold, 1874. Evergreen Cemetery.

Scroll. A scroll symbolizes the scriptures. Often the inscription is on the scroll as in the Anna Griswold marker.

Tree. The tree represents life. The "Tree of Life" is an ancient symbol that has been used by many cultures and religions. It is referred to in Genesis **2**:9. The most intense expressive symbolism on a gravestone in this area occurs on the Elizabeth Norton stone in the Old Durham Cemetery. Three trees are present on the lunette the first tree having been cut down. A cloud is present in the upper left. An arm bearing an ax emerges from the cloud and is poised over the fallen tree. In early Christian art, the countenance of God was never depicted. However, the presence of God could be shown as an arm or hand emerging from the clouds. This image symbolizes the hand of God descending from heaven and cutting short the life of Emily Norton represented by the fallen tree. The large tree in the center may represent the Tree of Life and the tree to the the right is Emily's husband. Another interpretation is that the tree in the center is Emily's husband and the smaller tree on the right is a child. This gravestone with its image is sandstone and is about to underdo delamination. It is unfortunate that there seems to be no practical means to preserve this remarkable example of early American art and symbolism. Legal and ethical restrictions, in many cases based on good reasons, make it extemely difficult to remove a gravestone from a cemetery.

Elizabeth Norton, 1751. Old Durham Cemetery.

The Elwood D. Parmelee gravestone bears a tree that has been cut down. As with cut flowers, a fallen tree represents a life cut short.

Elwood D. Parmelee, 1844. Evergreen Cemetery.

Flower. Flowers represent the life of Man symbolizing the beauty and brevity of his life. The rose signifies Christ and the persistent bloom of the flower, His resurrection. The most intricate flowers are on nineteenth century gravestones of white marble that could be carved. A cut flower lies atop the Nora Marsh stone. A broken stem on the flower indicates the person's death. A broken bud as on the David Kelsey stone signifies the death of a child while a broken whole flower as on the

Henry Chittenden stone means the person was cut down in the prime of life. The Emily Lane stone has a beautiful carving of lily flowers, one with a broken stem. The lily is a symbol of purity and chastity.

Nora Marsh, 1881. Union District Cemetery.

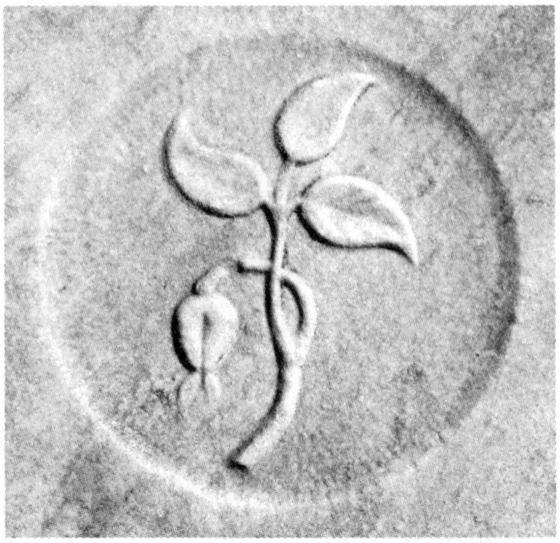

David Kelsey, 1861. Parker Hill Cemetery.

Henry Chittenden, 1892. Evergreen Cemetery.

Emily Lane, 1855. Lane District Cemetery.

An especially beautiful and poignant carving of roses is present on the Emily Eliza Wilcox stone. The stage of development of the flower signifies the age of a person. A rose in full bloom signifies a young adult. A bud beginning to open represents an adolescent. Closed buds are young children. On the Wilcox stone, there is a rose in full bloom, two buds of different ages, a broken bud, and a broken rose. The broken rose in full bloom represents Emily who died at age 25. Nearby Emily's marker is a gravestone for John Ellsworth Wilcox, a son of Emily who died at 10 months of age. The broken bud probably represents John. The unbroken rose is most likely Emily's husband John L. Wilcox, while the other two buds are surviving relatives.

Emily Wilcox, 1844. Union District Cemetery.

Jonathan Kelsey, 1804. Union District Cemetery.

Fleur-de-lis. The fleur-de-lis is an ancient symbol and may represent a stylized flower. In Christianity, it represents the Holy Trinity. It was used in Killingworth mostly on footstones, such as the footstone for Jonathan Kelsey, but also on a few headstones.

Oak. Oak leaves signify maturity and a ripe old age, also power and authority. The acorn symbolizes prosperity and fruitfulness. The John Griswold stone has a carving of a log with oak leaves and an acorn. A few gravestones in the Evergreen Cemetery such as the Clarence Parmelee stone have an acorn and oak leaf design on the edges.

John Griswold, 1893. Parker Hill District Cemetery.

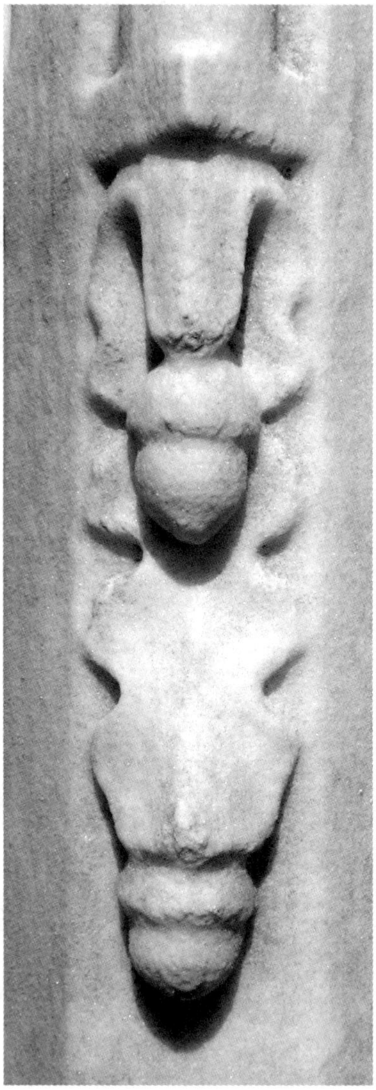

Clarence A. Parmelee, 1877. Evergreen Cemetery.

Wheat. A sheaf of wheat represents a soul ripe for the divine harvest which symbolizes the end of life. It is usually found on the gravestones of persons who lived a long and fruitful life of over 70 years. This example is seen on the gravestone of Heman Franklin. Heman died at age 58 and because he was a deacon of the Congregational Church, the wheat may signify the bread used in the Eucharist.

Heman Franklin, 1850. Union District Cemetery.

Book. A book on a gravestone is a representation of the bible. A bible opened to a page of scripture or an opened book as on the Clarence Parmelee stone represents the word through which one gains revelation. The writing on the book can be a simple message. A book occurs in the opening of the tapestry on the Mary Harris stone. A book can also represent a persons good deeds and accomplishments being recorded in the book of life. Bibles were used on the gravestones of pastors, as on the Rev. James D. Moore monument, deacons, or very devoted religious people.

Clarence A. Parmelee, 1877. Evergreen Cemetery. The Rev. James D. Moore, 1869. Indian River Cemetery.

"Be ye also ready." Mary Harris, 1848. Union District Cemetery.

Hand. The hand is an important symbol of life and represents the deceased's relationships with other persons and with God. Hands on gravestones are usually doing one of the following: blessing, praying, pointing, or clasping. A hand with the index finger pointing upward as on the Ella Parmelee and Sarah Dudley stones signifies the pathway to heaven. A finger pointing down represents God reaching down for the soul. A handshake as seen on the Mary Burr stone represents friendship and farewell to earthly existence. Clasped hands can also mean God's welcome to heaven.

Ella Orselia Parmelee, 1876. Evergreen.

Mary J. Burr, 1876. Parker Hill District Cemetery.

Sarah A. Dudley, 1858. Southwest District Cemetery.

Benny Lyne. Indian River Cemetery.

Bird. A bird is a messenger of God, signifying peace. The most common bird found on gravestones is the dove. The dove in Christianity represents the Holy Spirit. If it is flying, like on the Benny Lyne marker, it represents the flight of the soul and eternal life. The dove is carrying a bud representing Benny.

Lamb. The lamb signifies innocence, purity, and gentleness. It is found on children's gravestones as on the Susie Eliot stone. It also represents the sacrifice of Christ, the Lamb of God.

Susie Elliot, 1853. Indian River Cemetery.

Anchor. The anchor is seen most often on the gravestones of seafarers. The anchor is a symbol of hope well grounded. An anchor is seen on the Edwin A. Dibble monument. Christ is sometimes referred to as the anchor in the sea of life.

Musical Instrument. Musical instruments such as the harp, lyre, and flute can indicate heavenly music. A lyre is fund on the Elias Dibble stone. A broken string in the lyre signifies the loss of life.

Edwin A. Dibbell, 1907. Indian River Cemetery.

Elias M. Dibble, 1877. Indian River Cemetery.

Cross. The cross is the symbol most closely associated with Christianity. The Puritans, however, viewed it as a popish symbol and did not use it in their churches or on gravestones. It did not appear in this area until the second half of the nineteenth century in the form of gravestones and symbols on gravestones. It was popular in Catholic cemeteries as a symbol of faith in Christ's victory over death. The cross on the Elenor Hilliard marker is overlain with the branch of a palm tree. The broken branch may represent Elenor who died at a young age. Palm fronds also symbolize victory over death. A crown is above the cross. The cross on the Pratt monument is made of logs and has an ivy growing over it.

Elenor Hilliard, 1868. Indian River Cemetery.

Pratt monument. Indian River Cemetery.

Societies and Organizations. Many societies, organizations, clubs, and fraternal organizations have their own symbols that sometimes appear on tombstones. The most frequently encountered is that of the Masons. The primary symbol of the Freemasons is the square and compass. The letter G often occurs in the center and may stand for God, goodness, or geometry. The square and compass sybolize mind and matter and represent the progression from the material to the intellectual to the spiritual.

Nathan H. Clark, 1968.

Steadman Family, 1980.

Evergreen Cemetery.

Military. The gravestones of those who served in the militia or armed forces sometimes have military symbols. A pair of crossed swords occurs below a crown on the Capt. Nathanael Sutlief gravestone in the Old Durham Cemetery. Crossed swords usually occur on the markers of officers or indicate death in battle. The J. W. Parks stone in the Indian River Cemetery has a shield, a wreath signifying the victory of redemption, and crossed bayonets. Parks was killed at the battle of Antietam on September 21, 1862. The gravestone in the Union District Cemetery for George Marsh who also died in the Civil War bears a flag. The marker for Howard Hull who was in the U. S. Air Service has wings and a propeller. The cannons on the Charles V. Parker monument signify that he was in the Artillery. Other military symbols are the rifle, bugle, and ship.

Captain Nathanael Sutlief, 1760. Old Durham Cemetery.

J. W. Parks, 1862. Indian River Cemetery.

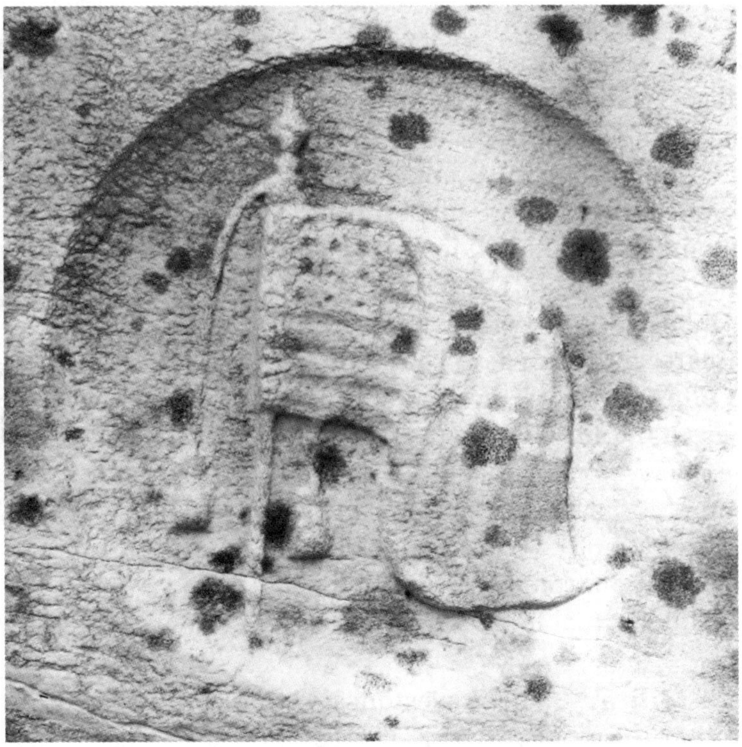

George Marsh, 1863. Union District Cemetery.

Lieut. Howard Brainard Hull, 1918. Evergreen Cemetery.

Charles V. Parker, 1899. Indian River Cemetery.

Statue. Statues are rare in Killingworth cemeteries but a very fine one of the Virgin Mary stands in the Preisig family plot in the Stone House District Cemetery. The statue signifies devotion to that holy figure and desire for their aid to attain heaven.

Priesig Family plot. Stone House District Cemetery.

Epitaphs

Epitaphs began to appear in the second half of the eighteenth century and are common on Killingworth nineteenth century gravestones. They appear below the inscription and consist of verses, poems, or eulogies. They were written by ministers, friends, or the families themselves. Some were general in nature and used frequently as on the Ebenezer Redfield stone and Josiah Redfield stone. Examples of a familiar warning are seen on the Mary Harris and Lucy Lester stones. Some, such as on the Philetta Hull and Dorinda Harris stones, indicate that death has released the person from suffering. Some verses are addressed to the deceased as on the Ella Parmelee, Ezra Rutty, and Lydia Franklin stones. On the Laura Parmelee stone, the departed child speaks to her parents. Some reveal something about the person or their death as on the markers for Concurrence Lord and Phinehas Spelman and the marker for Philander H. Hull who died in Alabama in 1837 and Calvin H. Hull who was murdered in Missisippi in 1848. Nathanael Sutlief was a Captain of the militia. Sad poems often occur on the gravestones of children as on the Rachel Evarts stone. Some epitaphs, as on the Ebenezer Robinson stone, are quite long and occupy the whole tablet.

Capt. Ebenezer Redfield, 1766. Indian River Cemetery.

Josiah Redfield, 1802. Southwest District Cemetery.

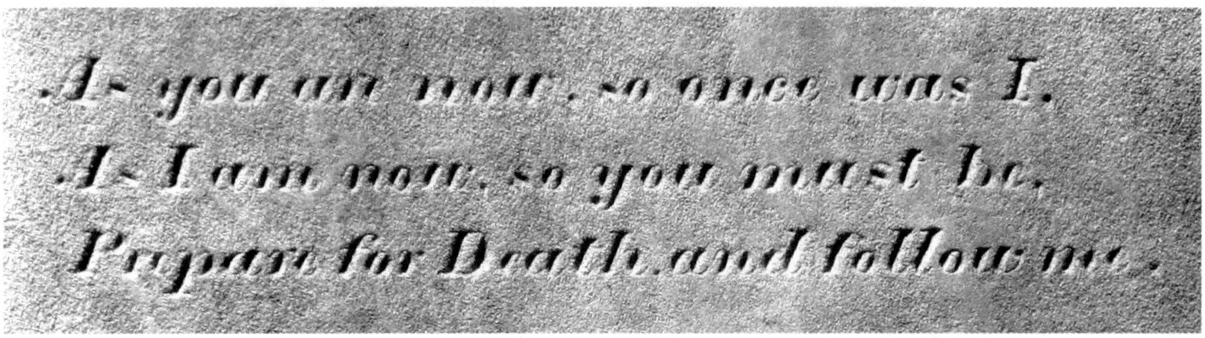

Mary Harris, 1848. Union District Cemetery.

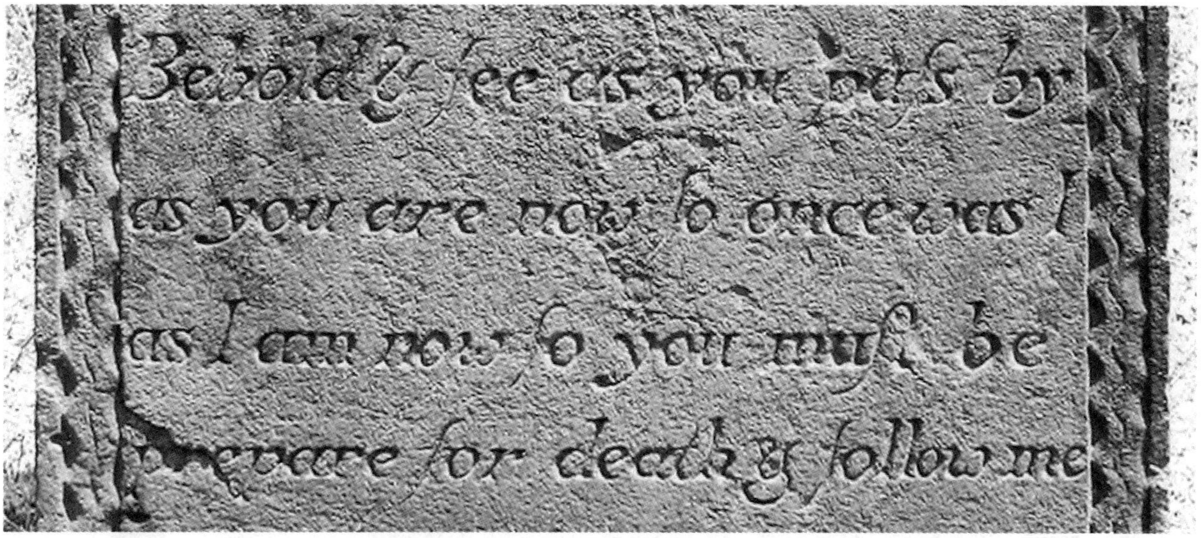

Lucy Lester, 1793. Indian River Cemetery.

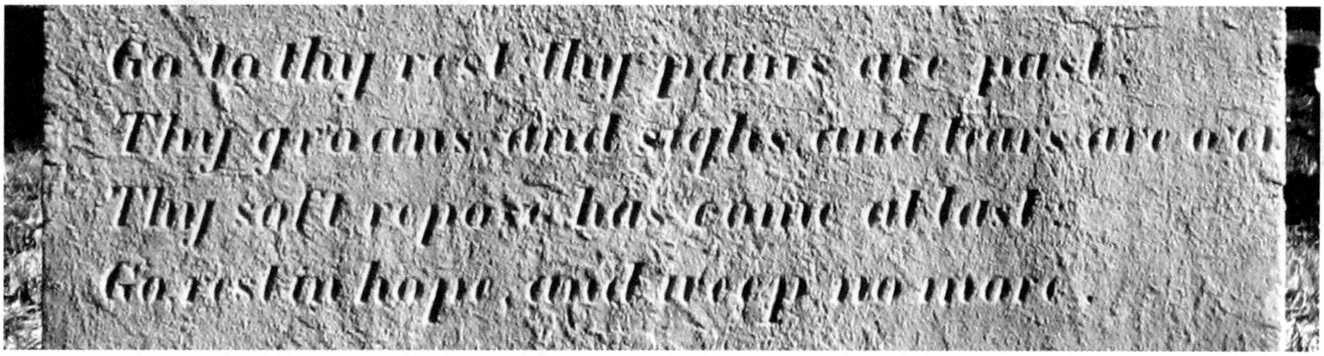

Philetta Hull, 1871. Parker Hill District Cemetery.

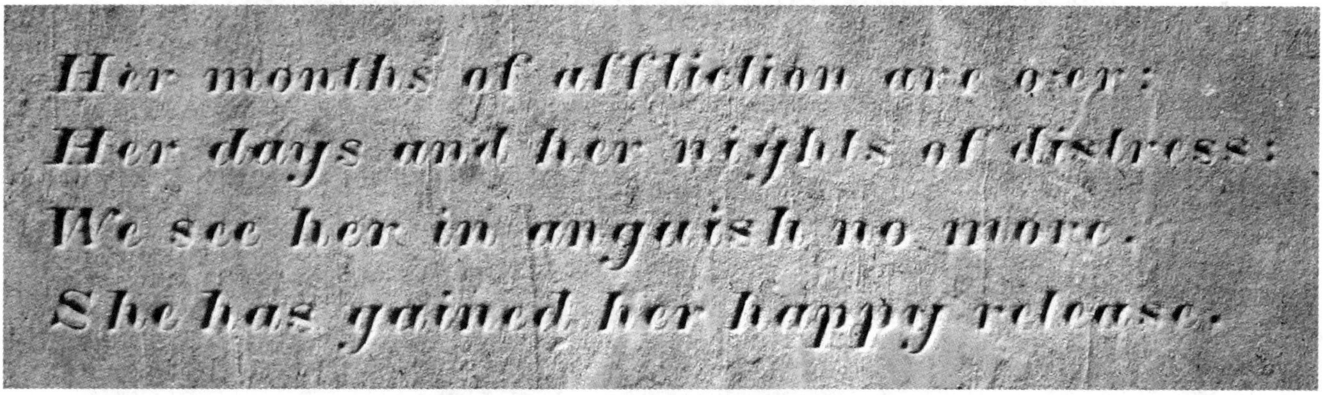

Dorinda Harris, 1845. Union District Cemetery.

Ella Parmelee, 1876. Evergreen Cemetery.

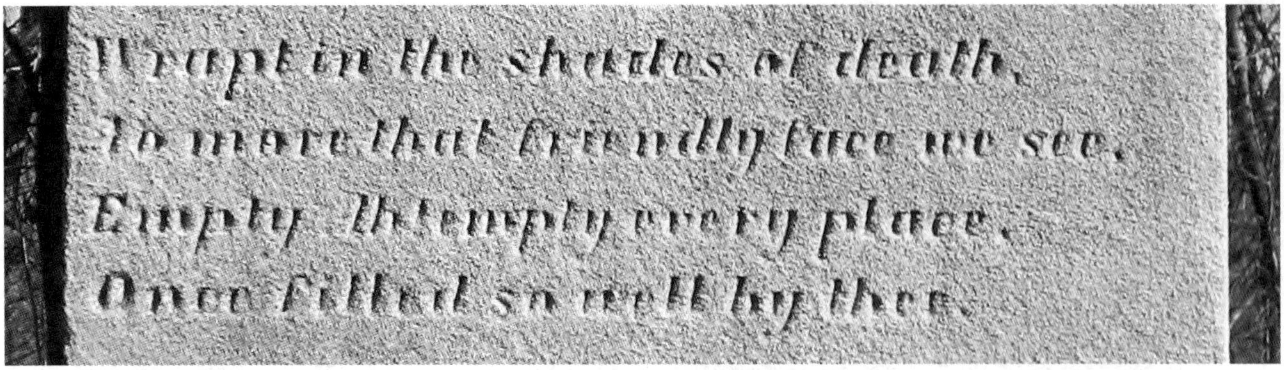

Ezra Rutty, 1852. Parker Hill District Cemetery.

Lydia Franklin, 1845. Union District Cemetery.

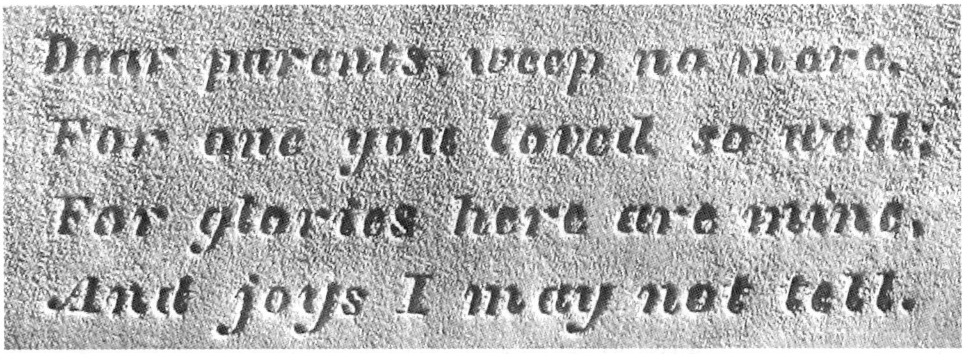

Laura Ann Parmelee, 1851. Parker Hill District Cemetery.

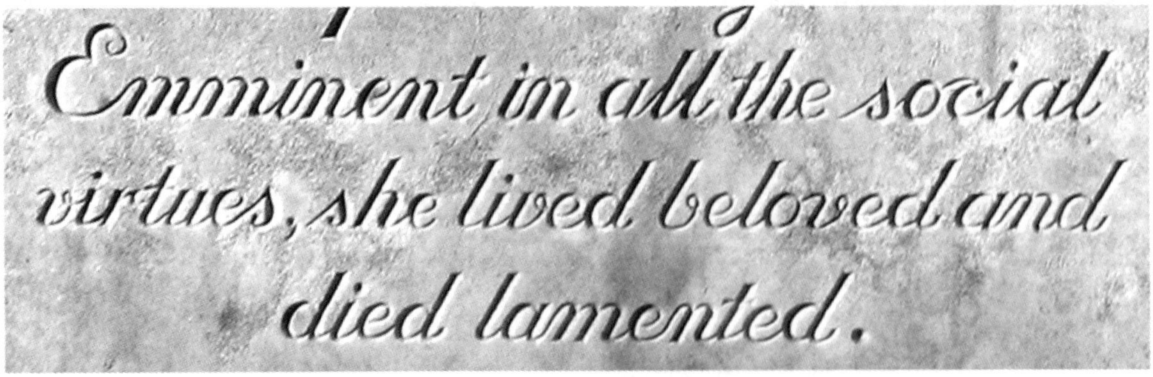

Concurrence Lord, 1799. Union District Cemetery.

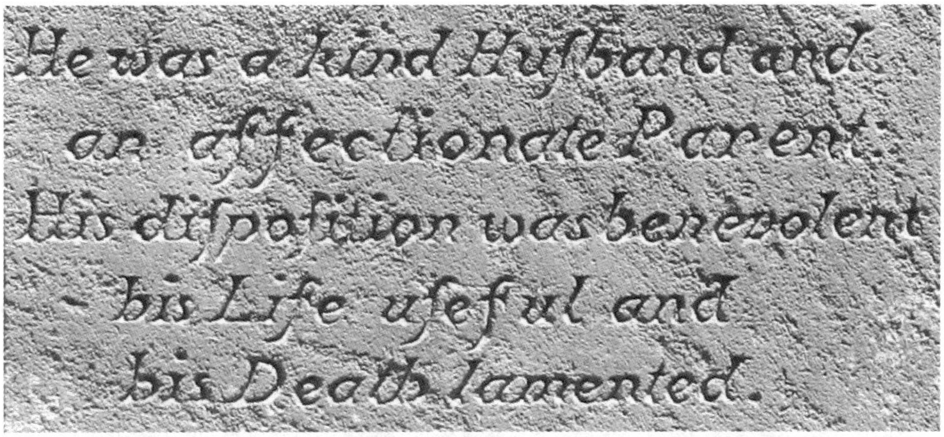

Phinehas Spelman, 1783. Old Durham Cemetery.

Philander, 1837, and Calvin, 1848, Hull. Parker Hill District Cemetery.

Captain Nathanael Sutlief, 1760. Old Durham Cemetery.

Rachel Evarts, 1876. Evergreen Cemetery.

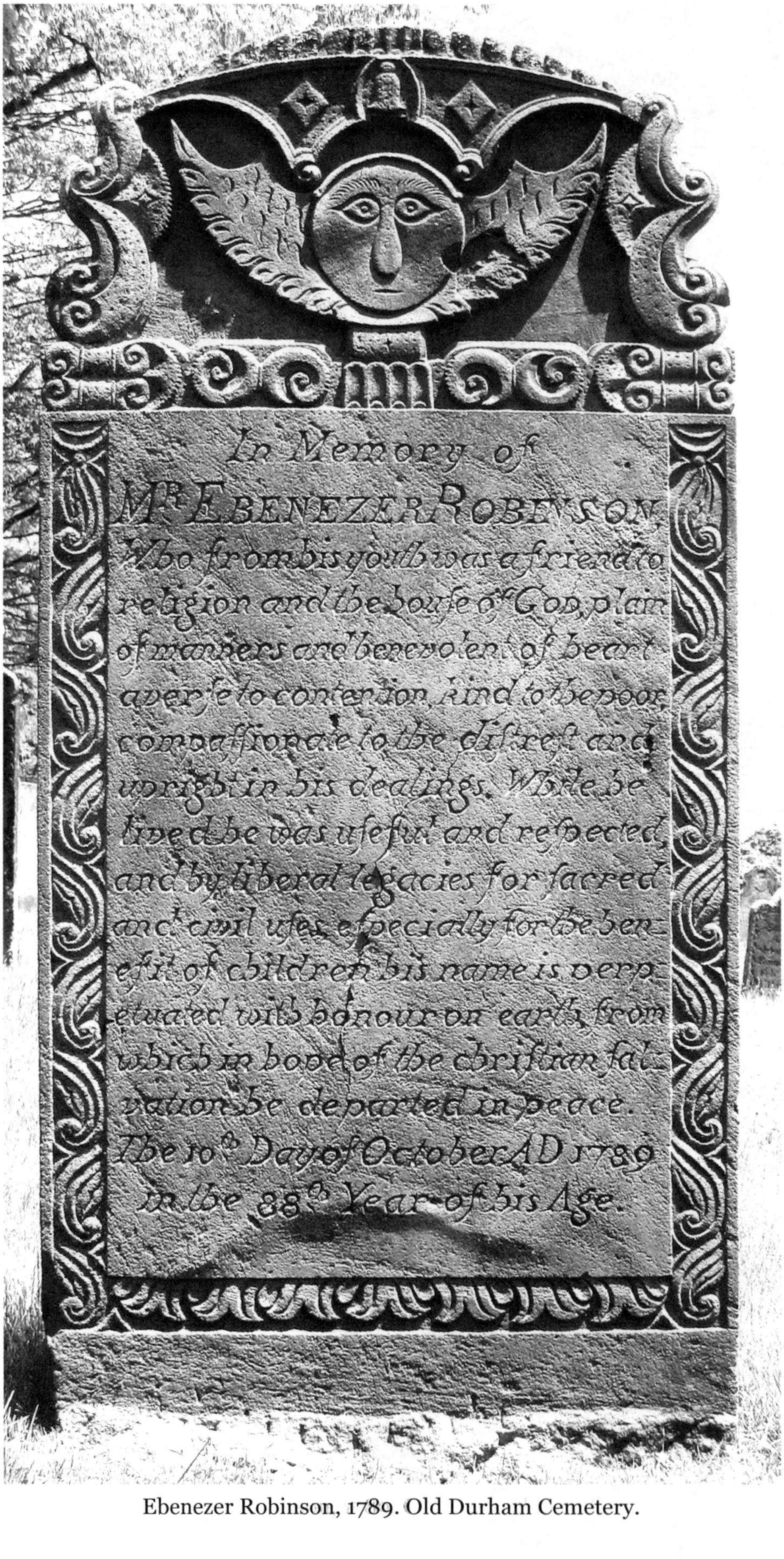

Ebenezer Robinson, 1789. Old Durham Cemetery.

Footstones

Footstones were placed at the foot of the grave. Like headstones, their carved surfaces faced outward from the grave so that a person would not have to stand on the grave to view them. Footstones are smaller than headstones and are made of the same material and have the same style as the headstone but are not as elaborate. These pictures illustrate the forms of footstones arranged chronologically. As with headstones, the first footstones were fieldstones. Early markers were plain as on the John Lane stone, bore initials as on the Jeremiah Steevens, Daniel Clark, Bathsheba Clark, and Rebekah Willcoks footstones, or had the name as on the Lieut. Nathaniel Parmele, Bani Parmele, and Martha Wilcoks footstones. A fleur-de-lis type design appears on the Jonathan Willcoks (1761) footstone. It is present on footstones like the Benjamin Lord, Experience Willcoks, Deacon Dodo Pierson, Jonathan Kelsey, and many other stones for the next forty years. A few footstones are more elaborate and resemble headstones, examples being the Concurrence Seaward, Nathan Buell, John Pierson, and Benjamin Turner stones. These often bear the name, date, a soul effigy, and a border. In the nineteenth century, footstones became simpler and were usually made of marble. A few bear a name as on the Abner Parmelee stone. Some such as the Jonathan Kelsey and Helen Marsh stones bear initials but others are plain marble markers a few inches high with no lettering.

Fieldstone. Union District Cemetery.

Jeremiah Steevens, 1739. Union District Cemetery.

Bani Parmele, 1747.

Daniel Clark, 1751.
Union District Cemetery.

Lieut. Nathaniel Parmele, 1752.

Bathsheba Clark, 1753. Union District Cemetery.

Concurrence Seaward, 1753. Union District Cemetery.

Martha Willcoks. 1755. Union District Cemetery.

John Lane, 1755. Union District Cemetery.

Rebekah Willcoks, 1758.
Union District Cemetery.

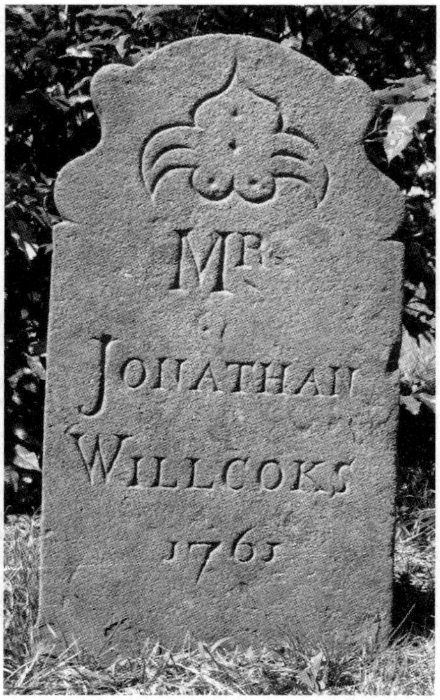

Jonathan Willcoks, 1761.
Pine Orchard District Cemetery.

Nathan Buell, 1770.
Union District Cemetery.

John Pierson, 1776.

Benjamin Turner, 1776.
Union District Cemetery.

Sarah Griswold, 1784.

Benjamin Lord, 1786.
Union District Cemetery.

Mary Lord, 1790.
Union District Cemetery.

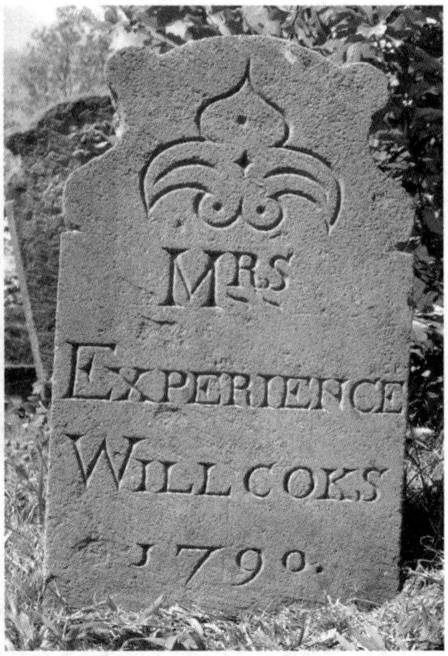

Experience Willcoks, 1790.
Pine Orchard District Cemetery.

Deacon Dodo Pierson, 1796.

Esther Lord, 1799.
Union District Cemetery.

William Lord, 1799.

Betsey, 1804, and David, 1803, Franklin.

Jonathan Kelsey, 1804.
Union District Cemetery.

Abner Parmelee, 1806.

Jonathan Kelsey, 1835.
Marble.
Lane District Cemetery.

Helen M. Marsh, 1869.
7 ½" w x 3 ½" h.
Union District Cemetery.

Unknown.
Marble.
Lane District Cemetery.

The Killingworth Area Graveyards

The Indian River Cemetery in Clinton is the original Killingworth Yard. Because Killingworth once included part of Durham, some examples from the Old Durham Cemetery are shown. There are eight cemeteries in present Killingworth, only one of which is in use. There appears to be no official listing of the names of the Killingworth cemeteries and, for some, different names have been used over the years. Some are now commonly known by the name of the road on which they are located. However, based on references to graveyards in the old town records, it appears that the names were meant to correspond with the historical school districts in Killingworth. Thus, the names used for the town cemeteries are Union District, Southwest District, Pine Orchard District, Stone House District, Lane District, Parker Hill District, and New Pine Orchard District (Emmanuel Church) Cemeteries. The Evergreen Cemetery is owned by a private association. In 1977, a columbarium interment ground known as The Rev. Milton R. Liebe Memorial Ground was established behind the Congregational Church. Examples of headstones in the cemeteries are illustrated in alphabetical order of the names of those buried. Names are spelled as on the gravestone. In the case of gravestones with initials, it is sometimes possible to identify the person based on the plot in which the gravestone is located and from vital records when a date is given on the stone. For the Killingworth cemeteries, all of the eighteenth century gravestones whose inscriptions are legible are shown. Some gravestones appear in other chapters. Representative examples of different types of later stones are shown.

Most of the early cemeteries in Killingworth are located on a small sandy plot of land that drops off on one or two sides into wetlands. These sites were not simply a case of choosing land unsuitable for farming when locating the burying ground. When the glaciers retreated, they left a blanket of till that covered bedrock hills and valleys. The till consisted of mixtures of clay, sand, gravel and boulders. Over the years, rain washed the sand and clay out with the clay settling into low lying ponds and lakes and the sand forming adjacent beaches. These sandy regions were chosen for burying grounds because the sand was much easier soil in which to dig graves. Thus, the Union District Cemetery, for example, is actually located on a sandy "beach" next to an ancient lake.

Most of the graveyards were in use prior to the time they were officially established. The minutes of Town meetings provide some information on the graveyards and their maintenance. On November 3, 1845, it was "Voted that the Selectmen examine all the burying grounds in this Town and have erected such fences as they deem necessary." Periodically, there were votes directing the selectmen to place fences around all of the burying grounds. The purpose of the fences was to prevent livestock from entering the graveyards and damaging the stones. On November 2, 1846, "Voted that all cattle be restrained from going at large on the burying grounds." On November 1, 1847, "Voted that the Selectmen make an effort to raise funds by subscription to defray the expenses of the fence for the Burying ground in Union District . . . ."

A row of stone posts runs along Roast Meat Hill Road across the front of the Union District Cemetery. The posts supported a heavy chain that was often stolen and is no longer replaced. In 1849, it was voted to "prosecute all encroachments of pasturing the burying yard in the South West District." At a Town meeting on September 28, 1886, "Voted: That this meeting, and annually hereafter, shall appoint a suitable person for each public burying ground in this town, whose duty it shall be to open and fill graves or cause the same to be done." It was further voted that this person should cut all bushes and weeds growing in the burying grounds at least once a year. Each year, sextons were appointed by the selectmen to care for the burying grounds. Sextons were appointed into the middle of the twentieth century. As they went out of use, the burying grounds fell into disrepair. The town budget today includes funds for mowing the grass in cemeteries. Volunteers cut brush and clean and reset gravestones.

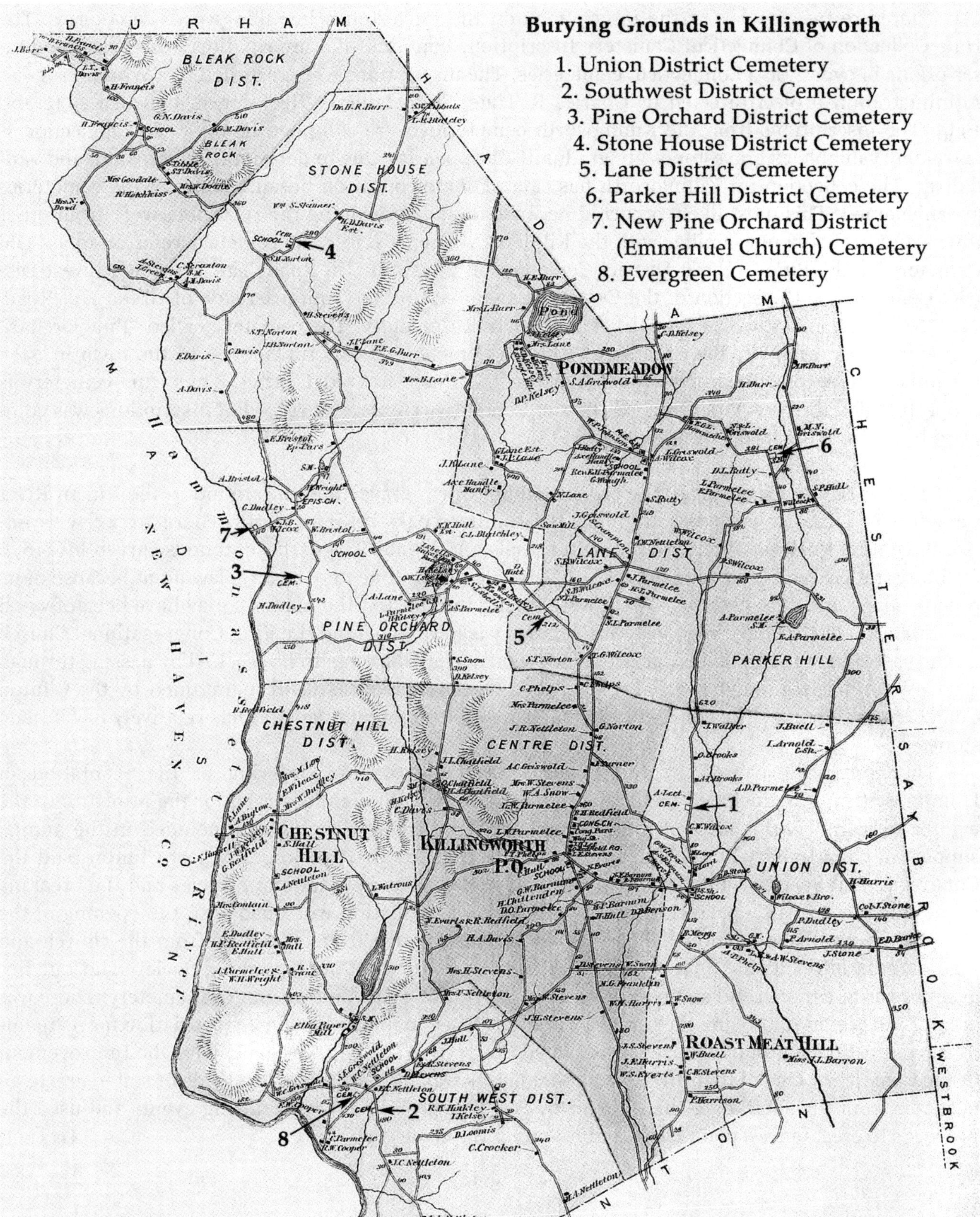

Burying grounds in present-day Killingworth.

There are two records of the inscriptions on the gravestones in Killingworth cemeteries. The Hale Collection of Connecticut Cemetery Inscriptions contains vital information from headstone inscriptions in over 2,000 Connecticut cemeteries. The inscriptions were recorded in a Works Progress Administration project directed by Charles R. Hale, State Military Necrologist, between 1932 and 1935. The inscriptions from the Killingworth cemeteries were compiled in 1934. This collection is extremely valuable as gravestones are gradually disappearing due to deterioration, erosion, and vandalism. The collection for Killingworth has caused some confusion because some of the cemeteries are misnamed. This most likely occurred because the persons doing the recording were from other towns and probably not familiar with the Killingworth cemeteries. The cemetery referred to as "Old Cemetery" is the Pine Orchard District Cemetery on Chestnut Hill Road. The "New Southwest District Cemetery" is the section of the Evergreen Cemetery on the southeast side of Green Hill Road. The "Nettleton Cemetery" is the Parker Hill District Cemetery. The cemetery called "Pine Orchard Cemetery" was originally the Emmanuel Church Cemetery. It was transferred to the town in 1948 becoming the second town-owned cemetery in the Pine Orchard District. Thus, this cemetery is properly called the New Pine Orchard District Cemetery. The second record of inscriptions was compiled by Glenn E. Griswold in 1936.

Indian River Cemetery. The earliest Killingworth gravestones are found in the Indian River Cemetery in Clinton, which was originally the southern part of Killingworth. There are a few seventeenth century gneiss markers carved with initials and a date. The earliest stone is carved MG 1670 for Margaret Griswold, the wife of Edward Griswold. This stone may be a replacement because of its precise shape and neat lettering. There were earlier burials, but the markers may have been of wood or simple stones that have been lost. The cemetery is located behind the First Congregational Church on the east side of the Indian River. It is somewhat secluded having to be reached by passing through a narrow underpass under the Amtrak railroad tracks. It is in use and maintained by the Clinton Cemetery Association. The cemetery is attractive and well maintained and has relatively few broken stones.

The committee chosen by the General Assembly for the ordering of the Plantation of Homonoscitt in 1663 included the Burying Ground in the allotment reserved for the Ministry. In the eighteenth century, the use and improvement of the Burying Ground was included in the annual support of the Ministry by the First Ecclesiastical Society. In 1842, the Town of Clinton paid the Congregational Society eight dollars annually to prevent the devastation of graves and the breaking of monuments by cattle pasturing in the cemetery. The situation worsened with the opening of the New Haven and New London Railroad in 1852. This separated the cemetery from the church and made access difficult. In 1854, a committee appointed by the Congregational Society laid out five avenues running north and south and two avenues running east and west in the cemetery. There was greater interest in improving the cemetery and the Town made an annual appropriation for its maintenance. In 1863, a group of citizens associated themselves as "The Association for the Improvement of the Cemetery." One of their first accomplishments was the carting of 500 loads of soil to create an entrance from the south over the railroad tracks. This group held fund raising events and used the proceeds to erect fences, plant trees, and maintain the cemetery.

Eleazer Baldwin, 1753.

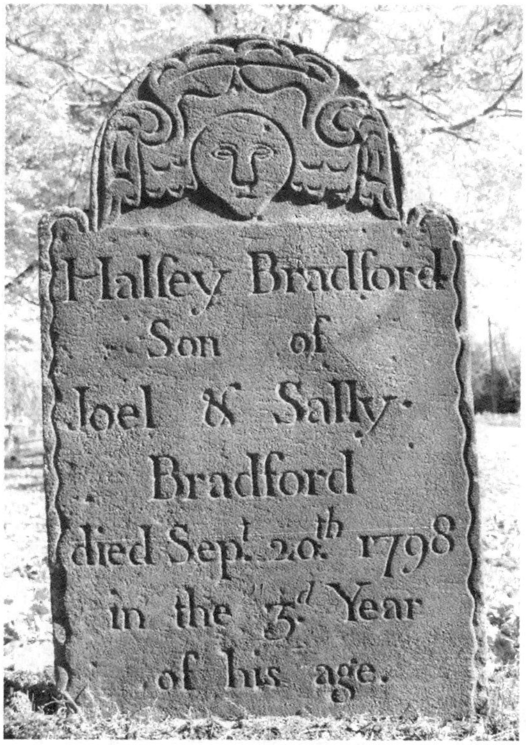

Halsey Bradford, 1798.

Lettered and dated Buell Family markers.

Benjamin Buell, 1723/4.

Louis Buell, 1758.

Deborah Buel, 1788.

Esther Buell, 1806.

Martha Buell, 1740. Slate.

Doctr. Reuben Buell, 1802.

John Butler, 1747.

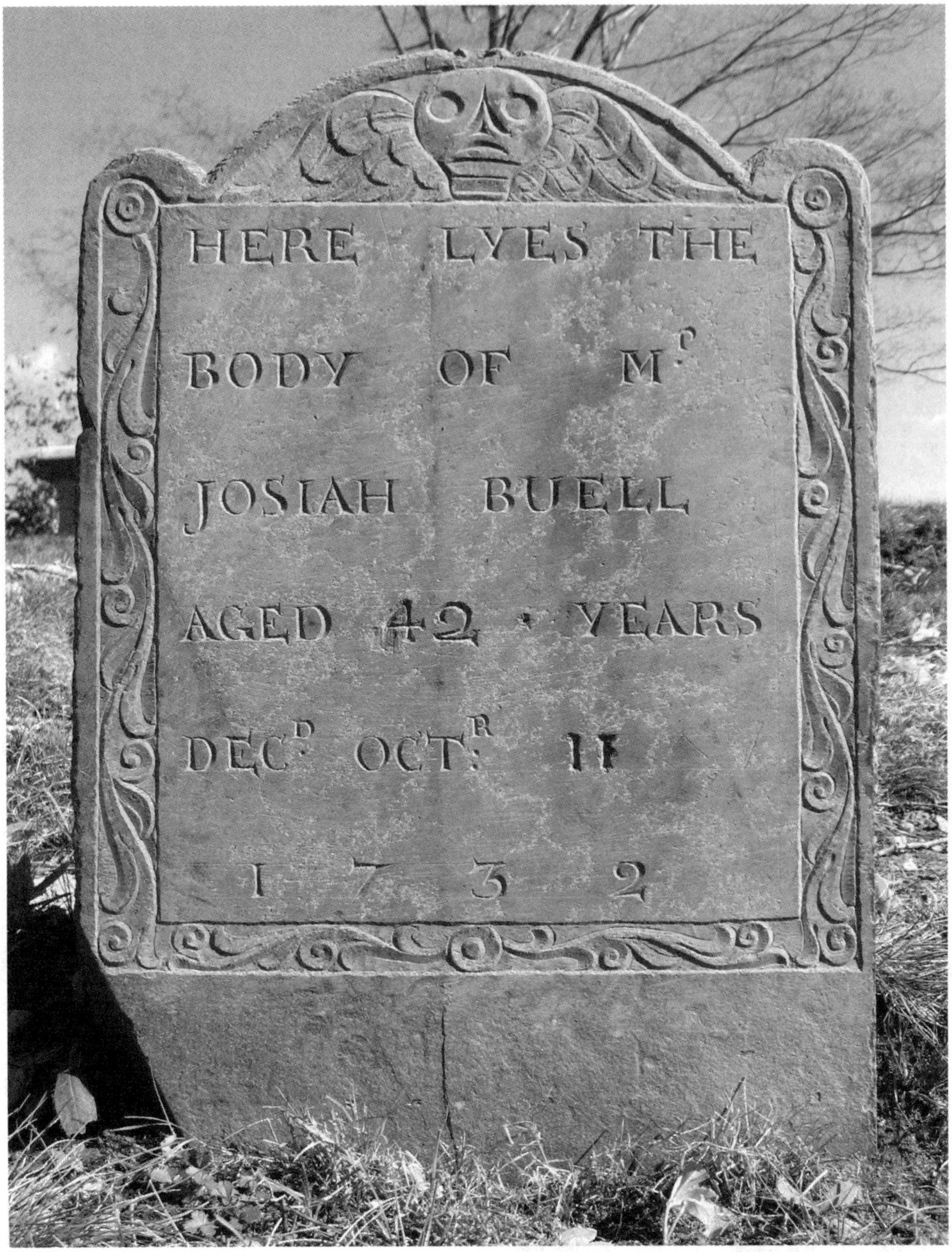

Josiah Buell, 1732. Slate, 16"w x 23"h.

"TB [Thankfull Buell], 1742."

Anna Crane [1732].

Elisebth Carter, 1738.

"1732, AGD 59, HC [Carter], W^{H}O DC SEPT 5."

John Chatfield, 1758.

Jane Crane, 1762.

John R. Crane, 1849.

Edwin A., 1897, and Mary M., 1912, Dibbell.

Simeon Crane, 1755.

Elias M. Dibbell, 1877.

Mary C. Eliot, 1909.

Nathan Eliot, 1757.

Sarah Eliot, 1769.

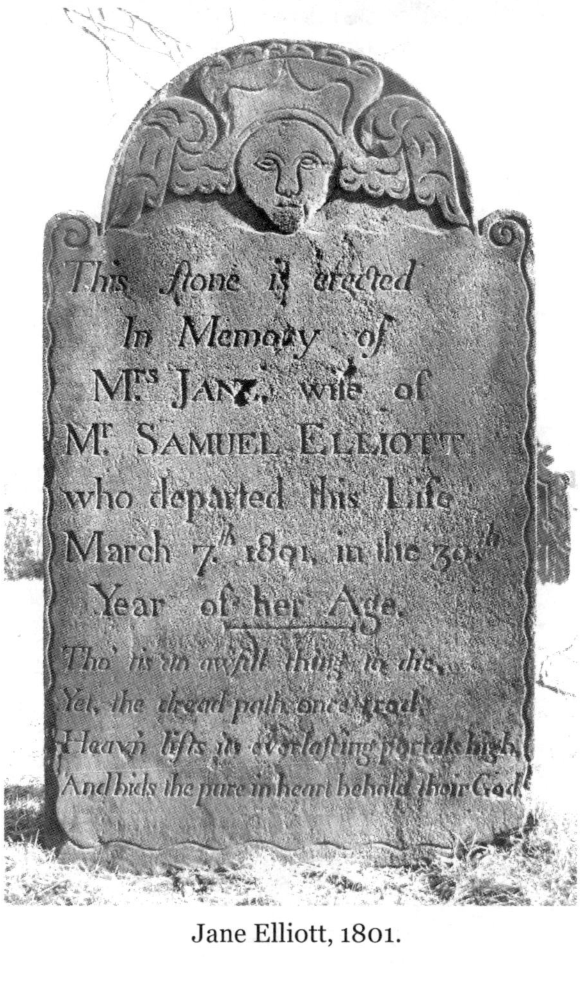

Jane Elliott, 1801.

Aaron Farnam, 1756.

Noah L., 1801, and Noah, 1802, Farnham.

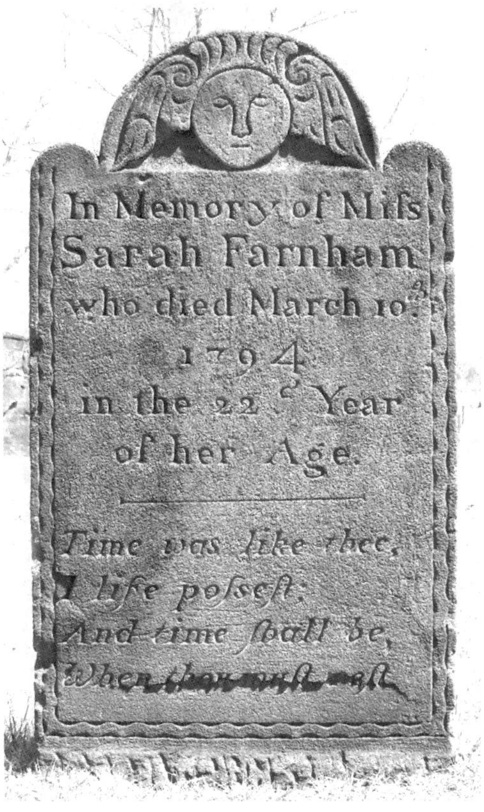

Sarah Farnham, 1794.

Daniel Gale, 1776.

Hannah Gale, 1797. Slate, 19 ½"w x 34"h.

Poolly Griffin, 1774.

Bathsheba Griswould, 1737.

"MG [Margaret Griswold], 1670."
Oldest dated marker, gneiss, 11"w x 34"h.

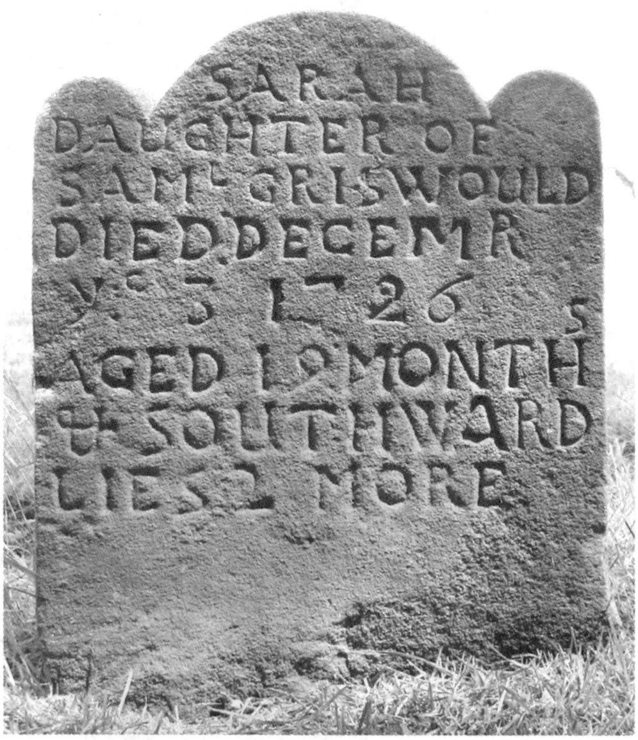

Sarah Griswould, 1726. Sandstone, 14"w x 18 ½"h.
"& SOUTHWARD LIES 2 MORE."

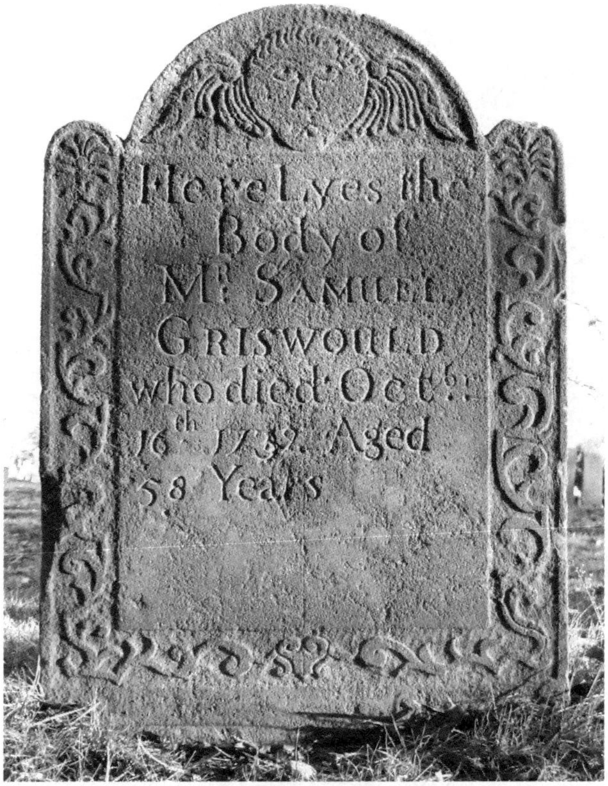

Samuel Griswould, 1732.

Martha Hilliard, 1796.

Charles E. Hillard, Lost At Sea, 1868.

Elenor M. Hilliard, 1868.

George Hull, 1755.

Juliana Hubbard, 1779.

Hannah Hull, 1751.

Hiel, 1867, and Une, 1869, Hull.

Samuel M. Hull Family monument, 1903.

Huntington infant son, 1767. Sandstone, 13"w x 19"h.

Abigail Hurd, 1799.

EH and RH, probably Ebenezer, d 1729, and Rachel, d 1730, children of Daniel and Rachel Hurd.

John and daughter Nabby Hurd died of smallpox in 1795.

Hurd Family monument. Granite.

"19 March MK [Mary Kelsey] D 1689."

Jehiel Kelcy, 1767. Sandstone, 17"w x 24"h.

Mary Kelcy, 1796.

Thankfull Kelcey, 1755.

Capt. Benjamin L'Hommedieu, 1755.

Hannah Lane, 1744. Sandstone, 14"w x 17"h.

Jonathan Lane, 1754.

Abigail, 1759, and Grace, 1796, wives of Capt. Noah Lane. Double stone, 37 ½"w x 45"h.

Capt. Jonathan Lane Esq., 1759. Sandstone, 23 ½"w x 38 ½"h.

Patience Lane, 1773.

Pacience, 1760, and Edward, 1765, Lane.

Silvia Lane, 1820.

John Lewis, 1752.

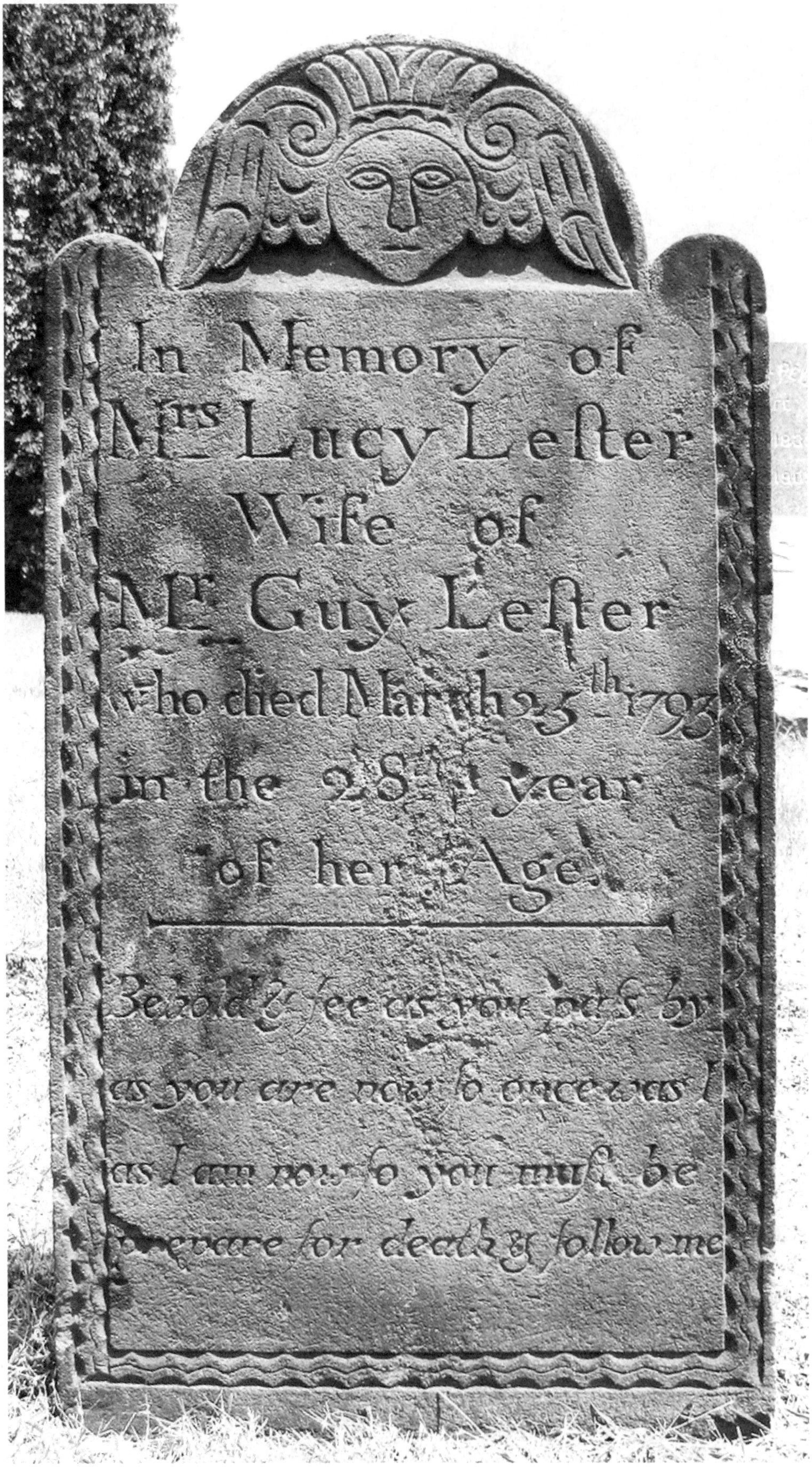

Lucy Lester, 1793.

Mary Lewis, 1765. Slate, 20"w x 32"h.

Benny Lyne. Marble.

Lizzie and Nellie Merrills, 1873.

Ebenezar R. Merrel, 1797.

Phebe Merrell, 1741.

Samuel Merrell, 1745

Rev. James D. Moore, 1869.

Jessie, 1872, and Thena, 1873, Moore.

"82 S P [Palmer] DIED LIES HERE."

Mary Morgan, 1768.

William Morgan, 1799.

Capt. Theophilus Morgan, 1766. Sandstone, 26"w x 45"h.

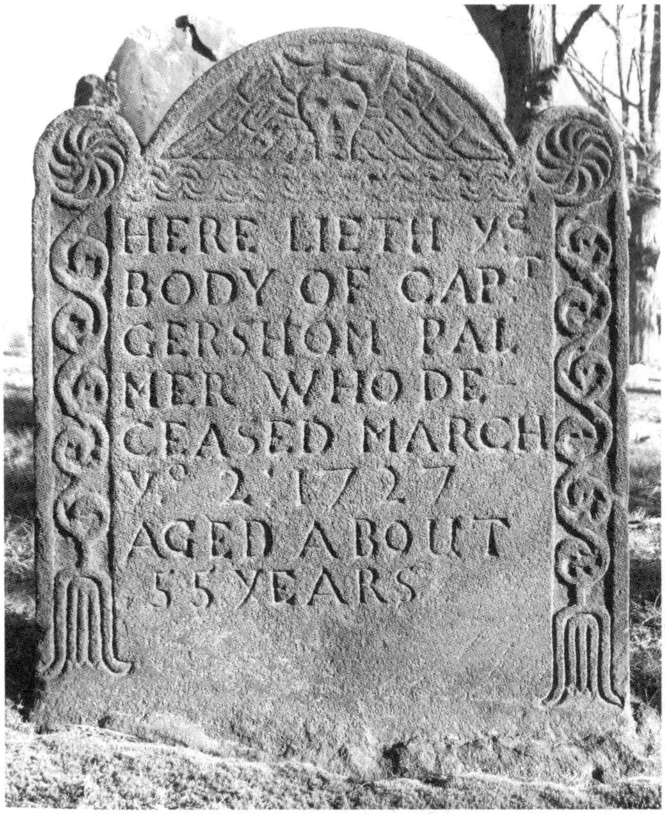

Capt. Gershom Palmer, 1727.

"N P 1712."

Daniel Peck, 1795.

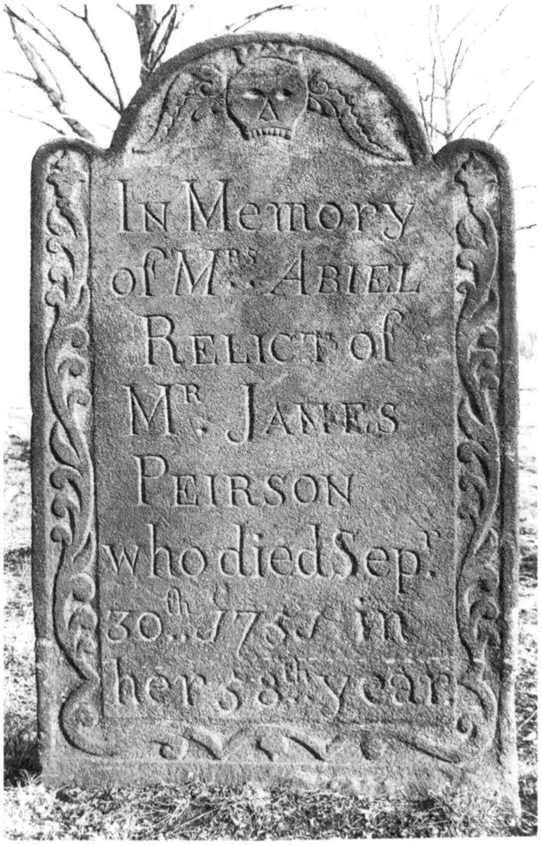

Abiel Peirson, 1751.

Mary Pierson, 1714.

Pratt Family monument.

Ens. Daniel Redfield, 1758.

Elizabeth Redfield, 1775.

Capt. Ebenezer Redfield, 1766. Red sandstone, 26"w x 46"h.

Martha Redfield, 1807.

Priscilla Redfield, 1770.

John Rossetter, 1801.

John Rossiter, 1841.

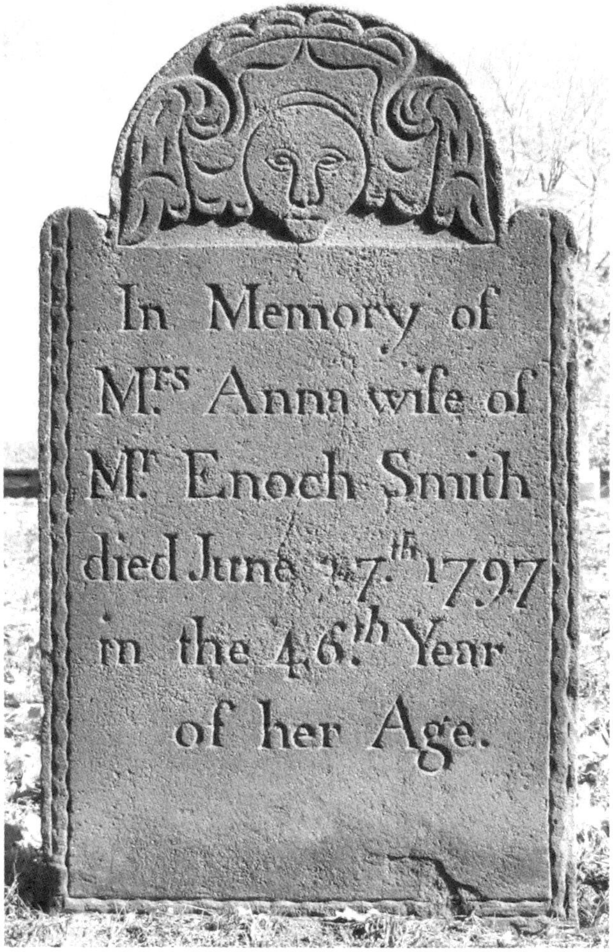

Anna Smith, 1797.

Abigail Spencer, 1778.

Elisabeth Steevens, 1748.

Dean. Phillip Stevens, 1814.

"C T 1687."

Nancy Trible, 1856.

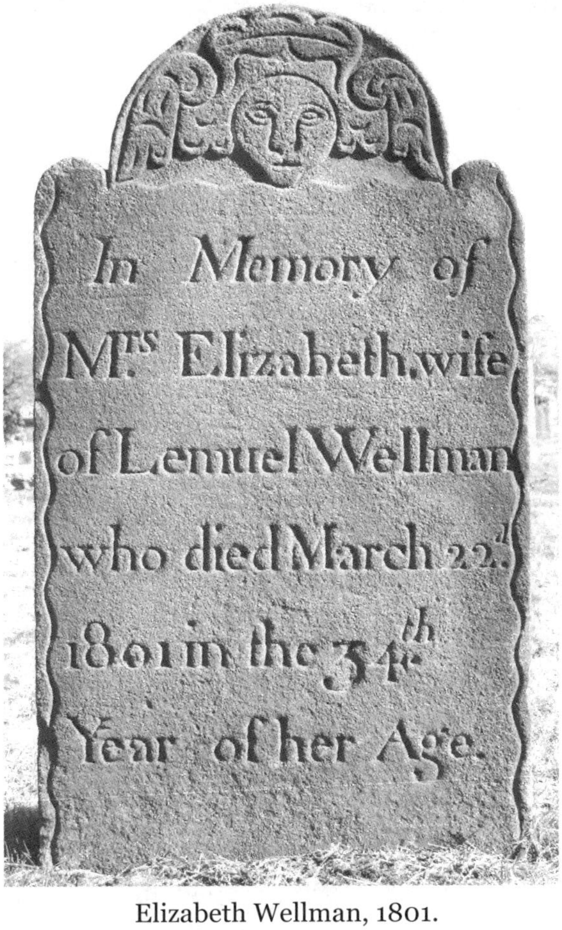

Elizabeth Wellman, 1801.

Elisabeth West, 1759.

Leut. Joseph Wilcoks, 1747.

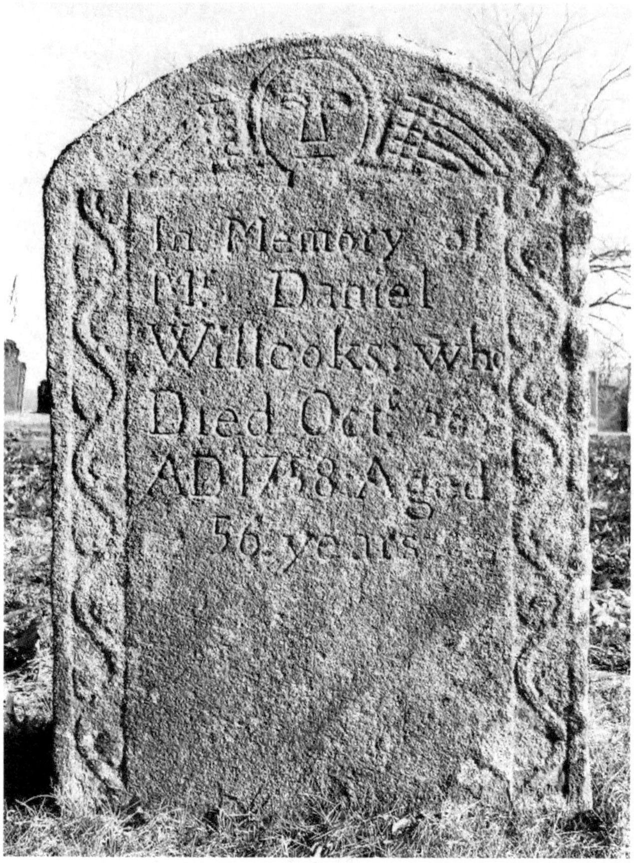

Daniel Willcoks, 1758.

Hannah Willcoks, 1730.

Samuel Willcoks, 1753.

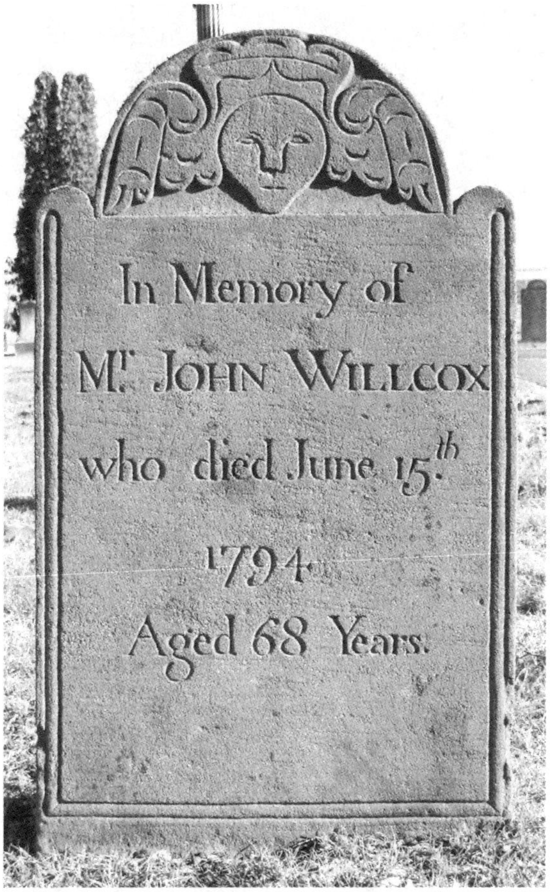

John Willcox, 1794.

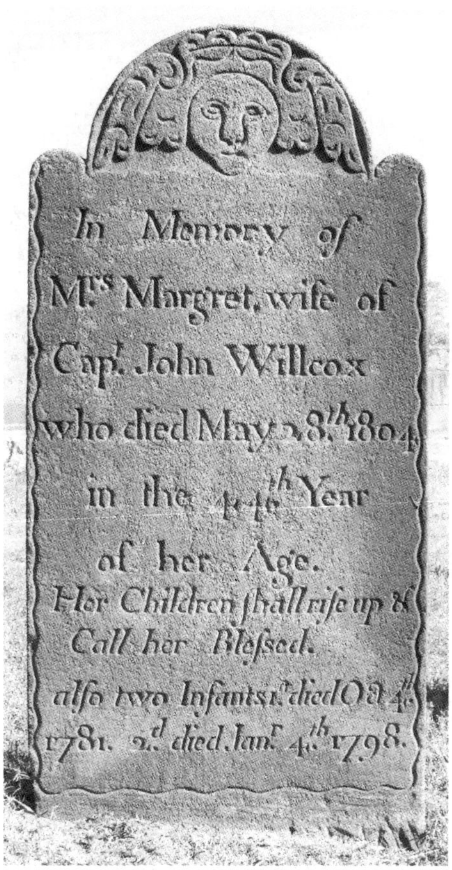

Margret Willcox, 1804.

Mary Willcox, 1795.

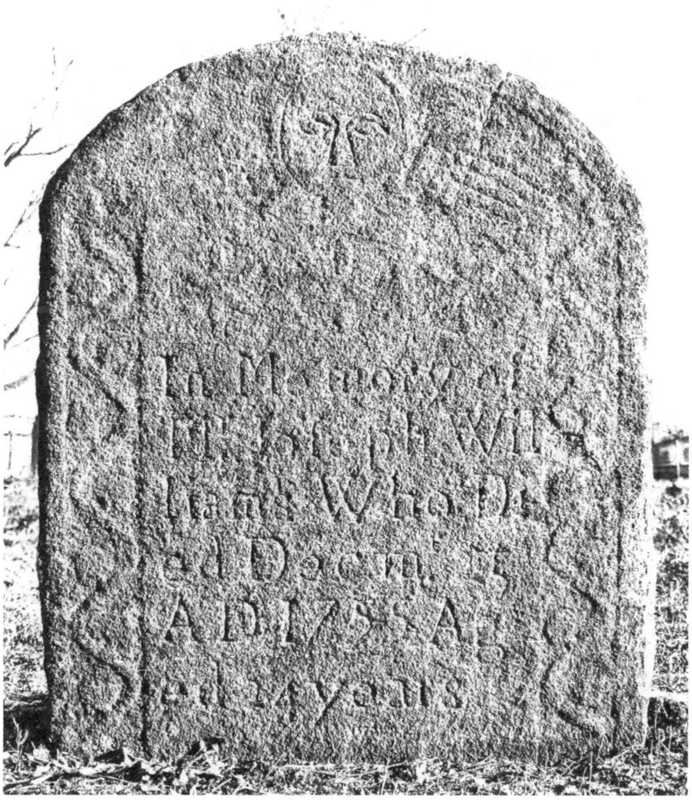

Joseph Williams, 1755.

Mehetabel Wilson, 1723.

Hannah Woodbridge, 1772.

James, 1727, and Hannah, 1719, Wright.

Gen. Horatio G. Wright memorial monument.

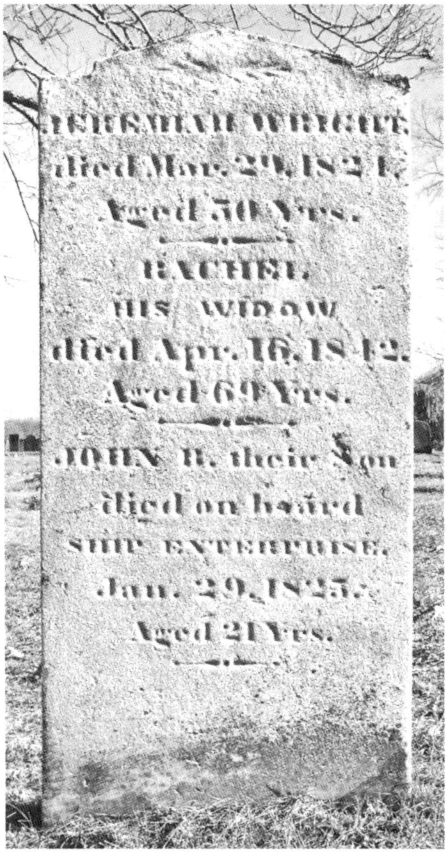

Jeremiah Wright Family.

Jeremiah Wright, 18"w x 25"h, 1727.

Louisa Cherrilla Wright, 1848.

Martin Wright, 1826. Marble.

Old Durham Cemetery. Durham has some close associations with Killingworth and part of the town was once a part of Killingworth. According to Field (1819), the Durham Yard was laid out in 1700. It is located on a steep hill facing Main Street. The Old Durham Cemetery has a large number of fine stones representing the changing styles of the eighteenth century. A few examples are shown here and many others are documented in the Farber Collection. There is considerable overlap between the gravestones in Durham and Killingworth as some carvers worked in both towns. However, many of the stones in Durham are more elaborate than those in Killingworth.

John Grant, 1736.

Steven Hickcoox, 1725. Sandstone, 20"w x 22"h.

Joseph Hickcox, 1725.

Noah Lyman, 1723. Sandstone, 20"w x 25"h.

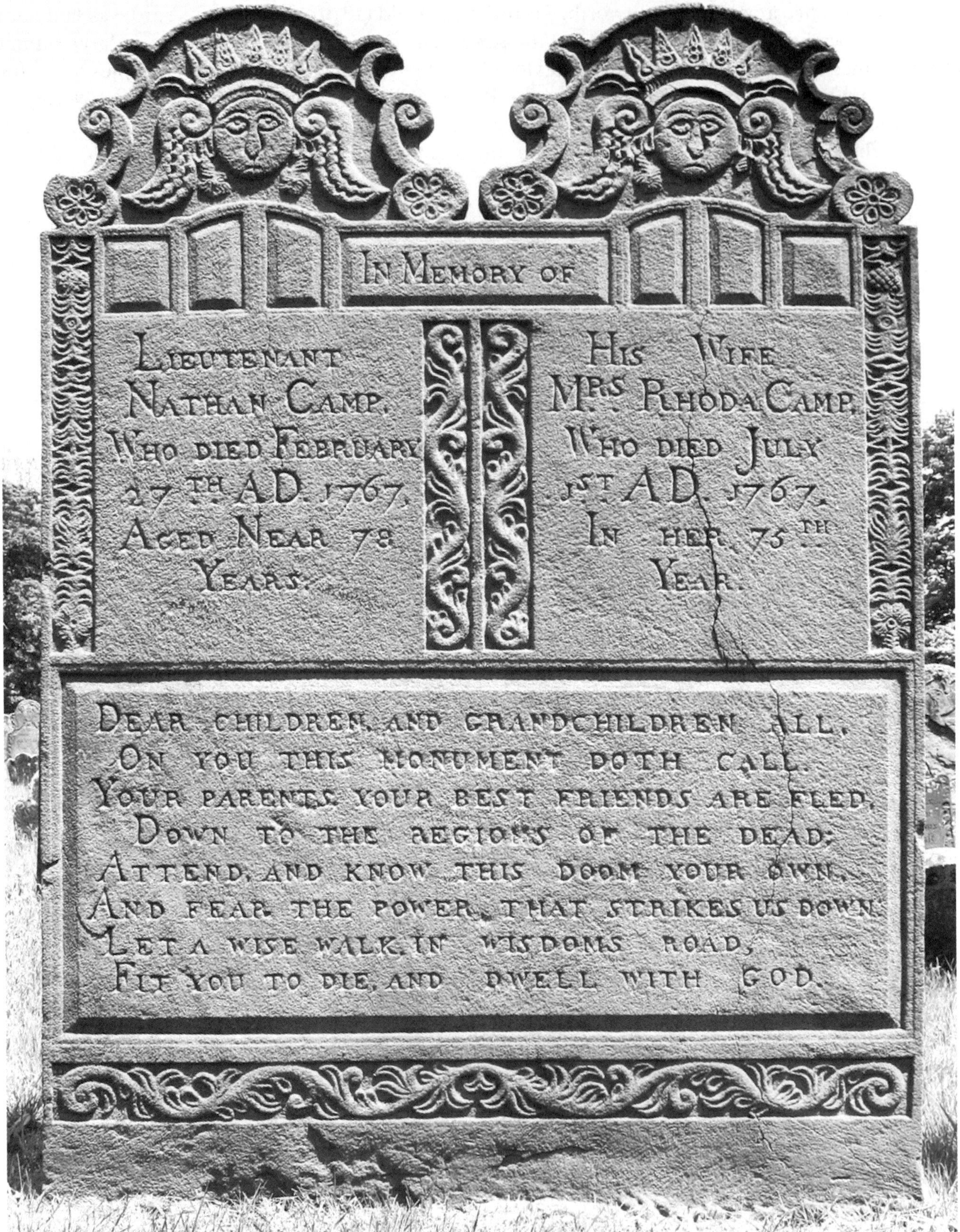

Nathan and Rhoda Camp, 1767. Sandstone, 48"w x 70"h.

Leutn. Samuell Parsons, 1734. Sandstone, 24 ½"w x 29"h.

Elizabeth Norton, 1751. Sandstone, 29"w x 49"h.

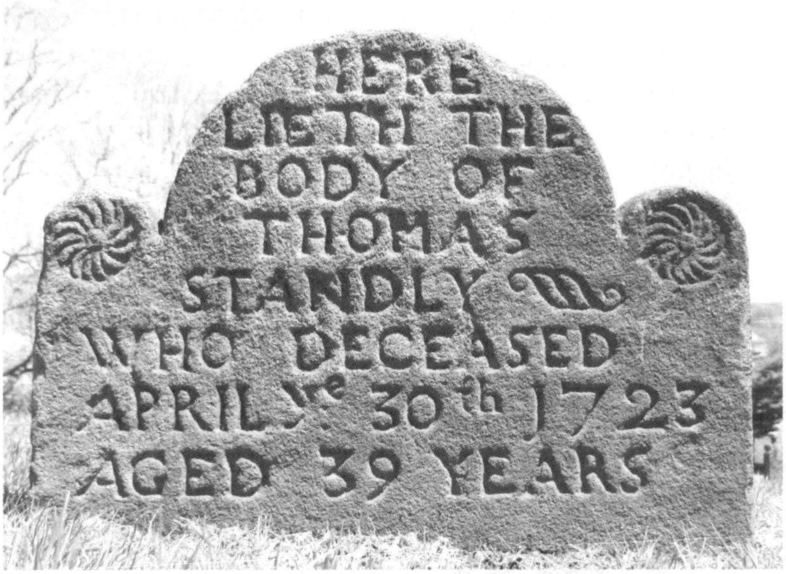

Thomas Standly, 1723. Sandstone, 20 ½ "w x 15"h.

Abraham Thomas, 1732.

Abigail Wadsworth, 1748/9. Sandstone, 30"w x 44"h.

Union District Cemetery. The Union District cemetery located on Roast Meat Hill Road is the oldest in present Killingworth. It was laid out March 22, 1738, although it is possible it was used earlier. In the rear of the Union District Cemetery, there is a double row of fieldstones that appear to be headstones and footstones. These may be the oldest markers in the cemetery. There are many other fieldstone markers in the cemetery. The gravestones of many of the first settlers, deacons, and patriots are located here. The oldest marked gravestone is that of Jeremiah Steevens, August 9, 1739. The cemetery is believed to contain the graves of three children who were murdered by their mother in October of 1779. Their locations are unknown although they could be the markers shown below. The cemetery was neglected for decades and fell into disrepair. Several very large spruce trees have grown up in the cemetery and give it a stately and haunting appearance. However, some of these trees fell during Hurricane Irene and other storms. The fallen trees crushed several gravestones. The Federal Emergency Management Agency (FEMA), through its Environmental Planning and Historic Preservation Program, provided funding for the removal of the fallen trees and repair of the broken gravestones. Remaining trees are being removed by the town as funds permit. Volunteers have reset many fallen gravestones greatly improving the appearance of this historic cemetery.

Gravestones damaged during Hurricane Irene.

Fieldstone headstones and footstones for children.

Fieldstone.

Shaped Fieldstone.

Plain Marker.

Hermann Broch, 1951.

The last burial in the cemetery is that of Hermann Broch in 1951. Broch was one of the leading European novelists of the first part of the 20th century best known for his work *The Death of Virgil*. He is considered one of the originators of the modern novel and was nominated for the Nobel Prize in Literature. He came to the United States after the annexation of his native Austria in 1938. Broch was a faculty associate at Yale University and a friend of Henry Seidel Canby, a Yale professor, author, and editor of the Saturday Review of Literature. Canby lived in Killingworth and when Broch died far from his homeland, Canby asked first selectman Raymond A. Griswold if it would be possible to inter the ashes of a friend in the Union District Cemetery. Griswold agreed and a granite marker was placed over the grave.

"E B 1747."

The EB stone is that of Esther, daughter of Daniel and Esther Buell, born December 2, 1746, died January 5, 1747. The stone is red sandstone and 14 inches high and 14 inches wide. It is crudely done with crooked guidelines and January spelled "JANeWary." The inscription also occurs on the back of the stone but is even cruder. The carver, probably a local farmer, must have decided to try again on the other side with only marginal improvement. This interesting little stone was found completely buried.

Gravestones harbor many organisms including various types of lichens, fungus, mold, algae, and moss. Most of the eighteenth century gravestones in Killingworth were covered with these growths making many illegible. With time, these growths cause the surfaces of the stones to deteriorate. The Elisabeth Buel gravestone is shown before and after cleaning. Instructions for cleaning gravestones are provided by the Connecticut Gravestone Network but it should not be done without training and permission.

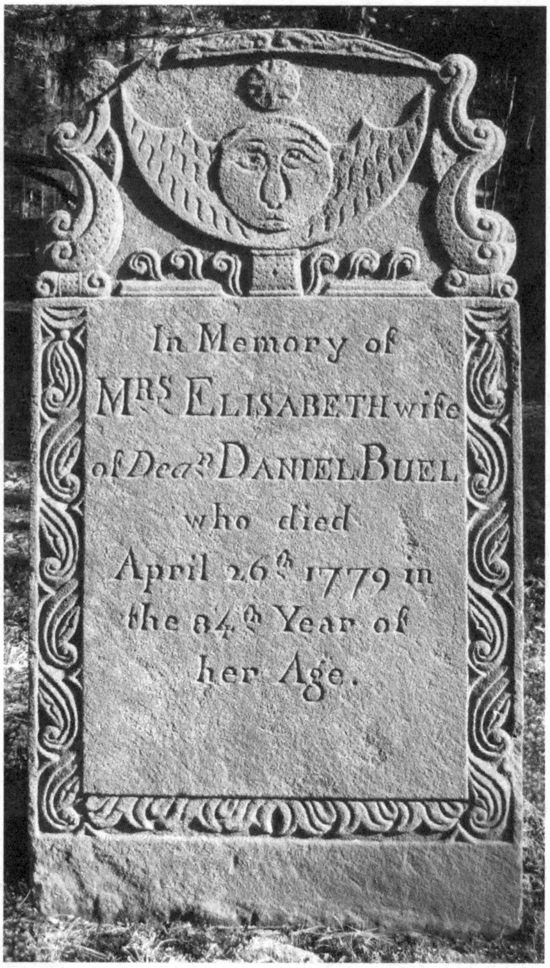

Elisabeth Buel, 1779. Before and after cleaning with water and a soft brush.

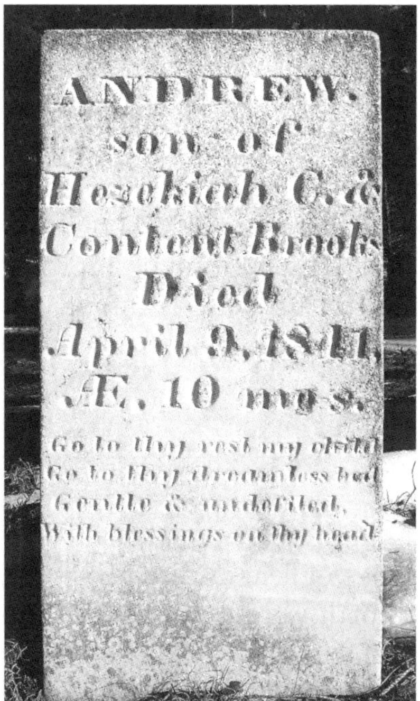

Andrew Brooks, 1841.

Hezekiah C., 1870, and Content N., 1879, Brooks.

Gordon Buell, 1745.

Thomas Clark, 1794.

Clark Family headstones and footstones in front and Seward Family markers in background.

Bathsheba Clark, 1753.

Daniel Clark, 1751.

Eliphelet Clark, 1752.

Samuel Clark, 1752.

Jehiel Evarts, 1792.

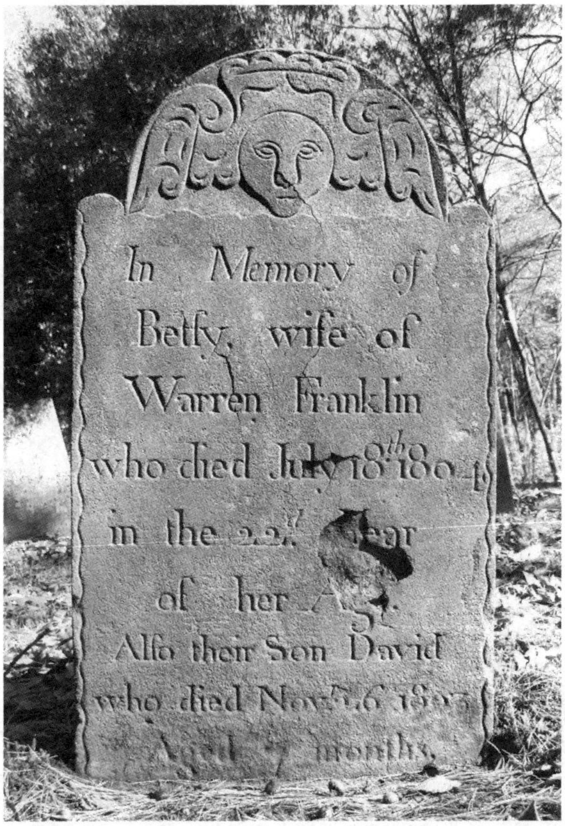

Betsy Franklin, 1804, and Son David, 1803.

Lydia M. Franklin, 1845.

Joel Gaylord, 1862.

Lucretia Griswold, 1788.

Michael Griswold, 1776.

Moses Griswold, 1822.

Nathan Griswold, 1826.

Noah Griswold, 1784.

Elizabeth Harris, 1800.

Jedediah Harris Esq., 1854.

Mary Harris, 1848.

Damaris Hull, 1803.

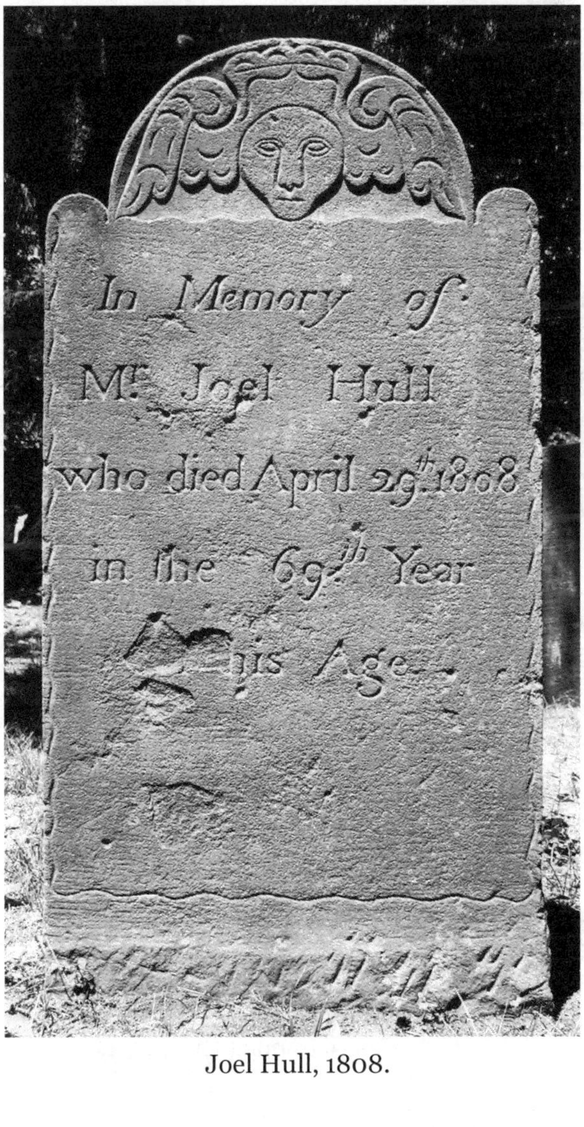

Joel Hull, 1808.

Captain Josiah Hull, 1753.

Nathan Hull, 1813.

Ens Nathanael Hull, 1751.

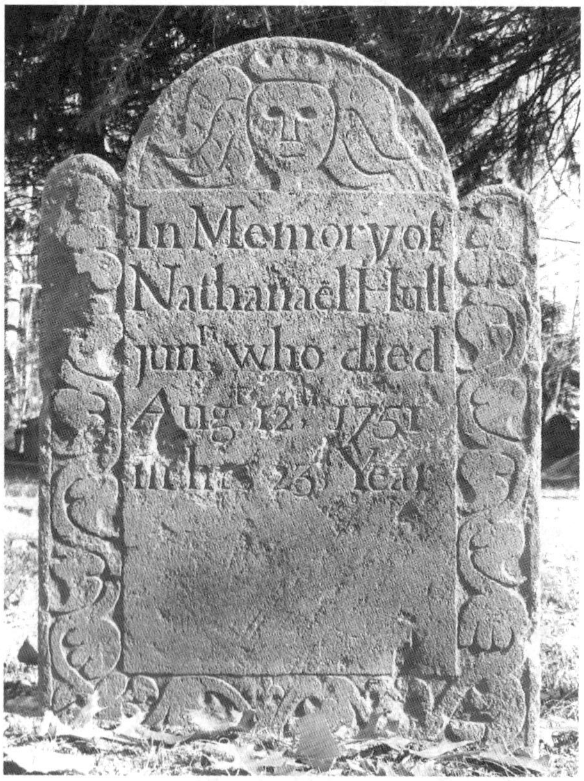

Nathanael Hull junr, 1751.

Hull Family obelisk. Roswell Hull, 1847; Irene Hull, 1870; Lucius Hull, 1864.

Elisabeth Hull, 1773.

Nathaniel Hull, 1753.

Jonathan Kelsey, 1804.

Mary Kelcey, 1772, and David Kelcey, 1794.

Joseph Kelsey, 1800.

Zerviah Kelsey, 1816.

Rebekah Kirtland, 1751. Gneiss.

Abigail Lane, 1824.

Elijah Lane, 1749. Gneiss.

Jabez Lane, 1836.

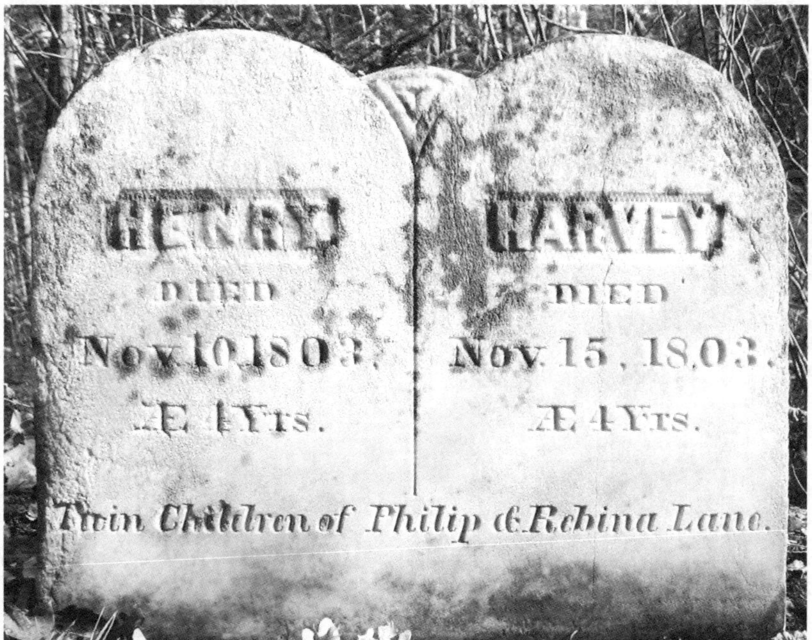

Henry and Harvey Lane, 1803.

Marvin Lane, 1797.

Mary Lane, 1813.

Benjamin Lord, 1786.

Charles Seward Lord, 1790.

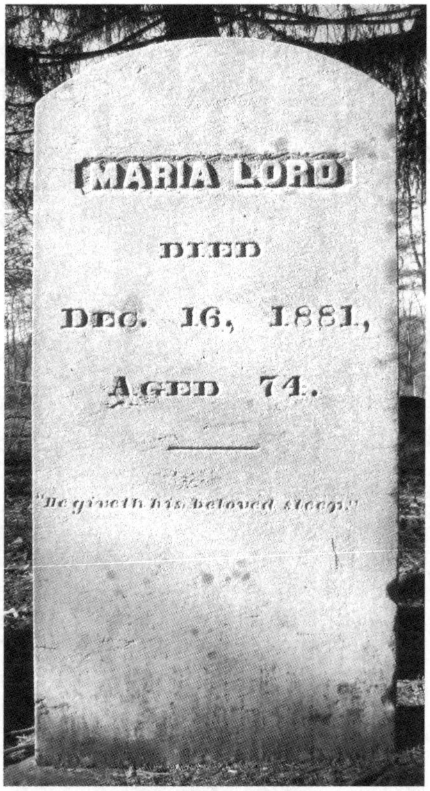

Maria Lord, 1881.

Martin Lord, 1889.

Mary Lord, 1790.

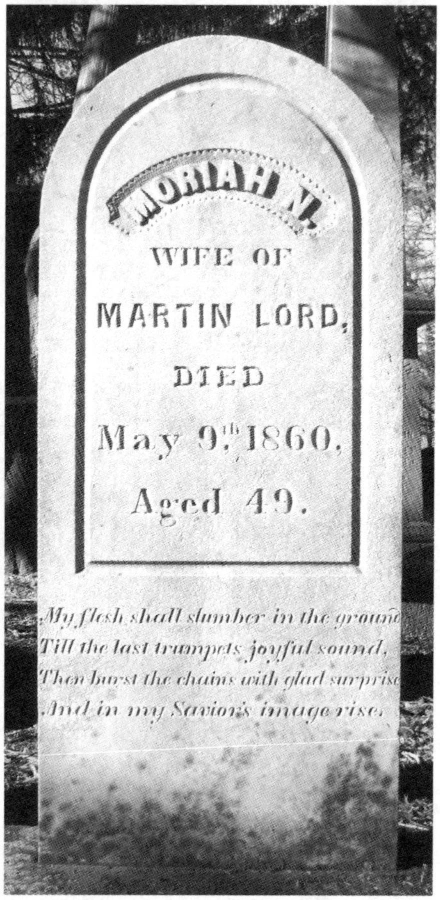

Moriah N. Lord, 1860.

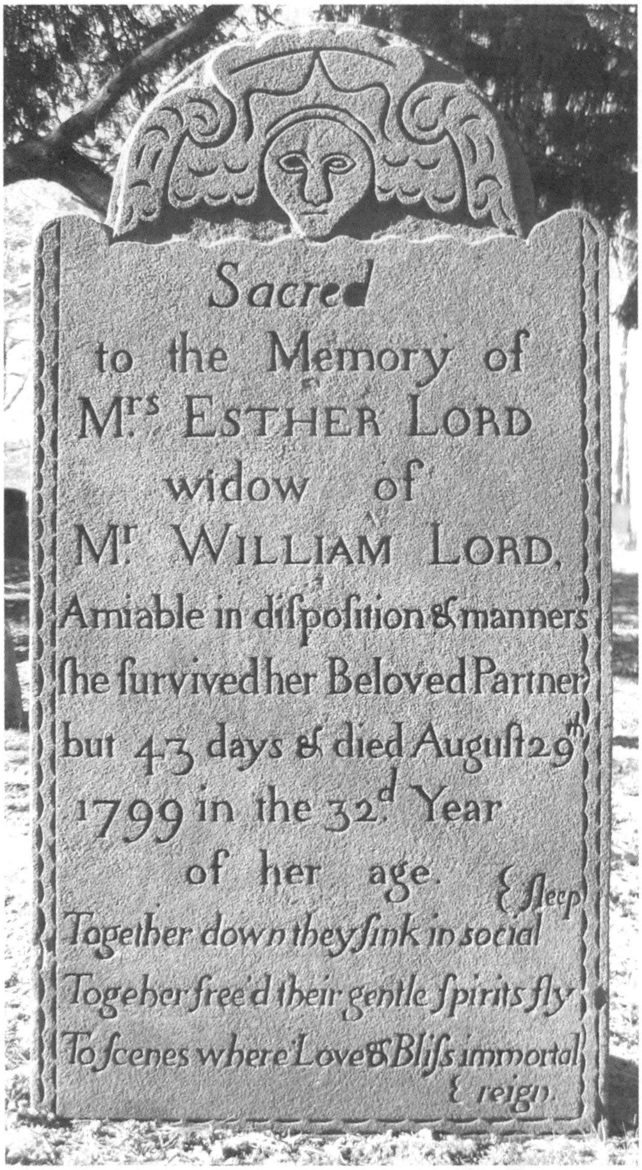

William and Esther Lord, 1799.

Nora Marsh, front and back, 1881. Marble.

Asahel Parmele, 1784.

Bani Parmele, 1747.

Eliab Parmele, 1799.

Mary Parmele, 1785.

Lieut. Nathaniel Parmele, 1752.

Rachel Parmele, 1787.

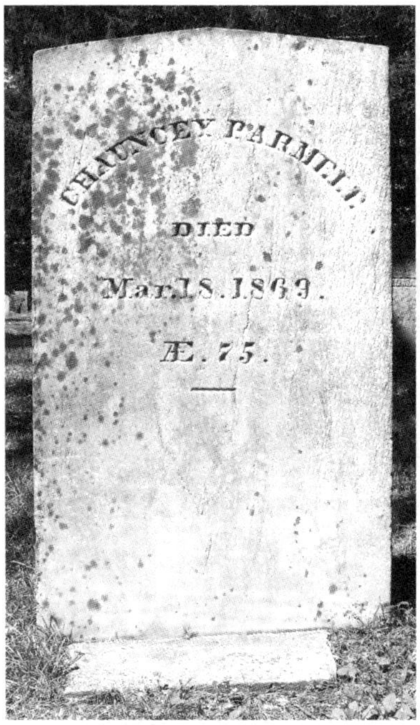

Chauncey Parmele, 1869.

Rhoda Parmele, 1806.

Solomon Parmelee, 1819.

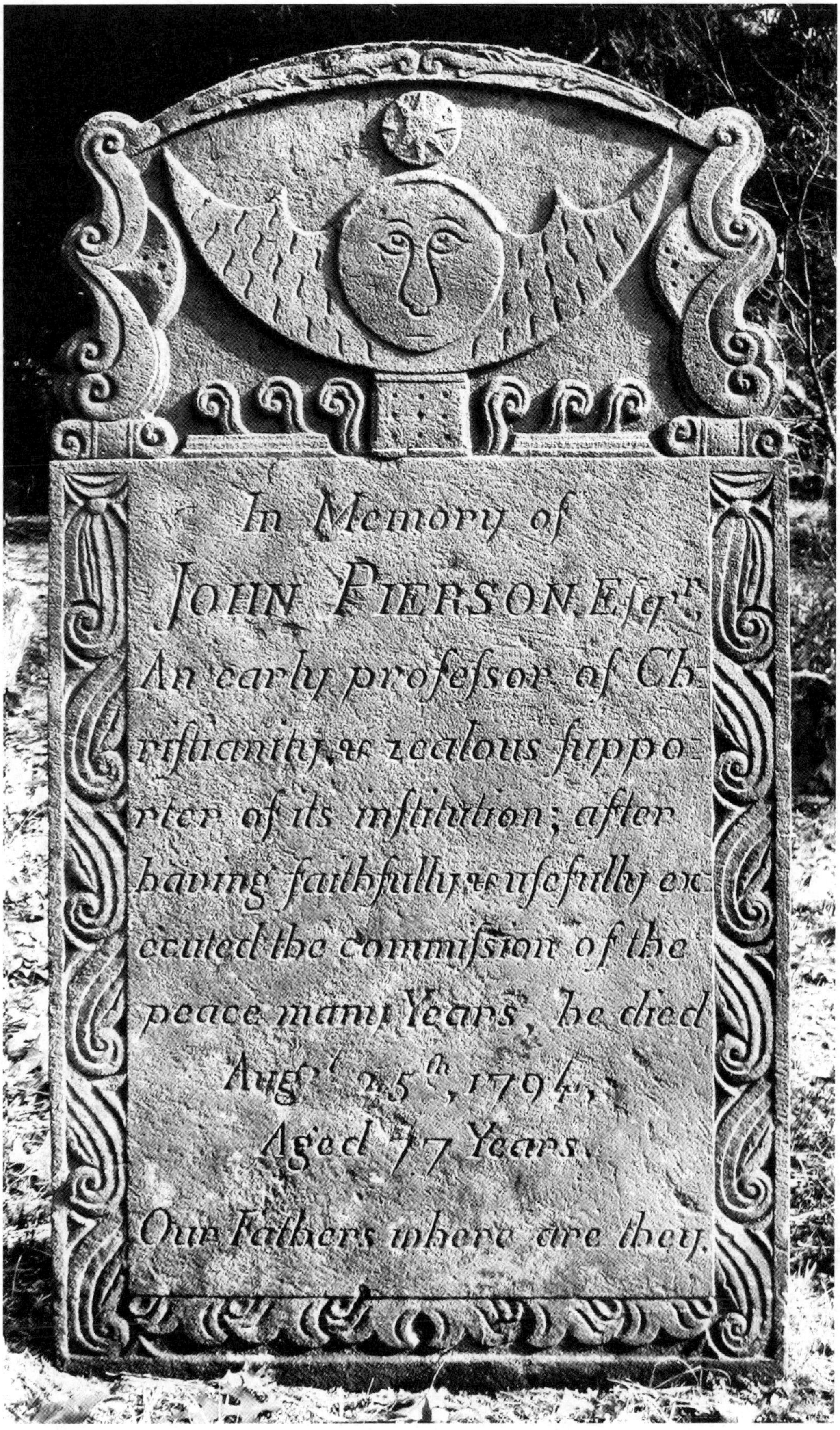

John Pierson, Esqr., 1794. Sandstone, 25 ½"w x 47"h.

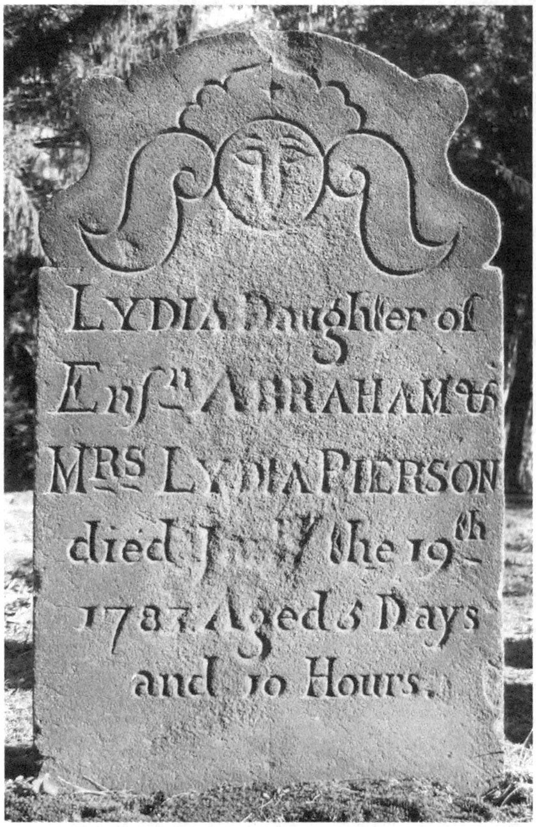

Lydia Pierson, 1787.

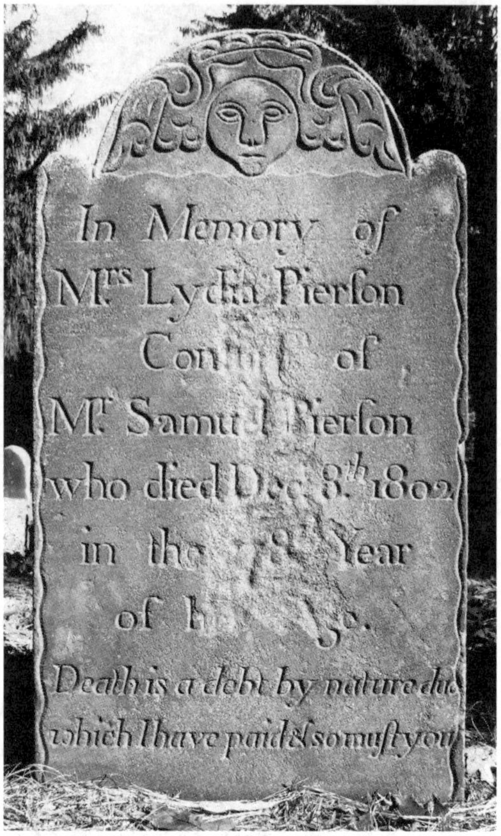

Lydia Pierson, 1802.

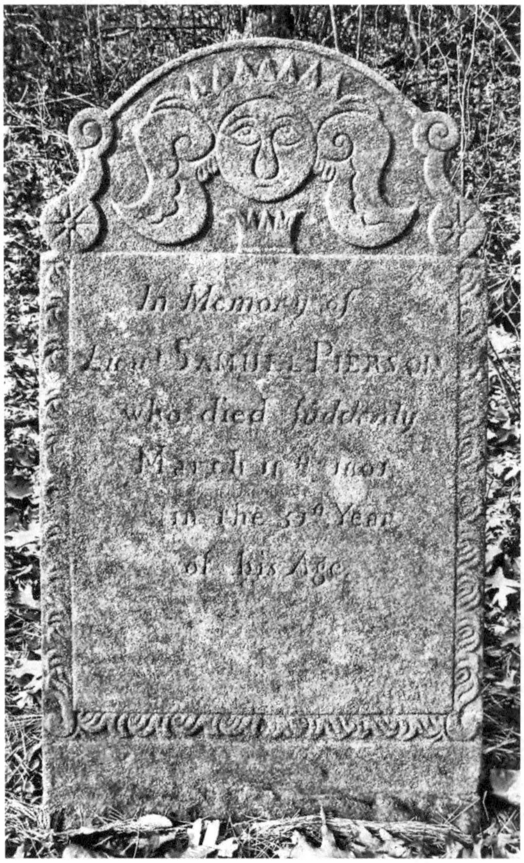

Lieut. Samuel Pierson, 1801.

Mary Pratt, 1798.

Hannah Rutty, 1808.

Levi Rutty, 1830.

"E S" [Stevens].

Jeremiah Steevens, 1739. Red sandstone, 22"w x 29"h.
Oldest dated gravestone in Union District Cemetery.

William P. Stevens, 1829.

Irene Stone, 1809.

Louis Stone, 1797.

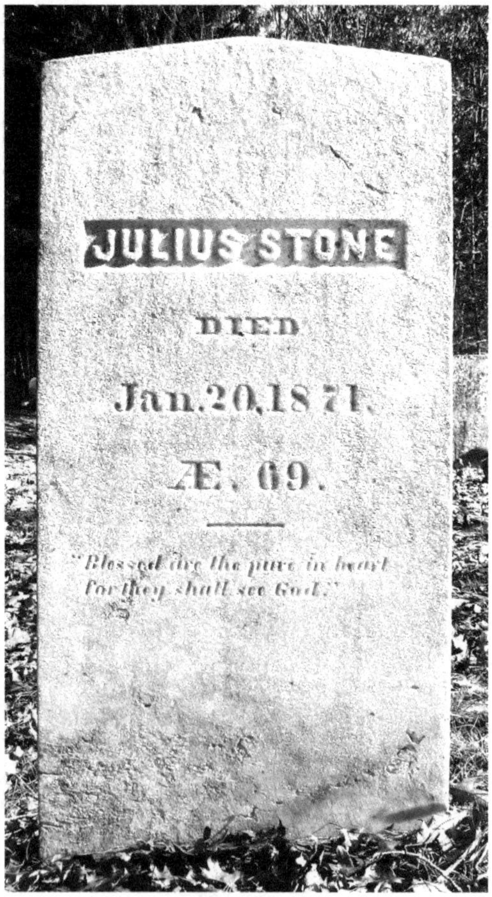

Julius Stone, 1871.

Martha Turner, 1751.

Martha Turner, 1752.

Abel Wilcox, 1784.

Emily Eliza Wilcox, 1844.

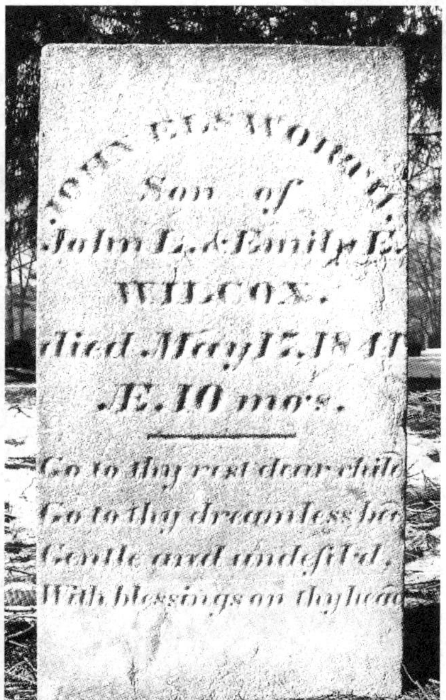

John Elsworth Wilcox, 1841.

Martha Wilcox, 1776.

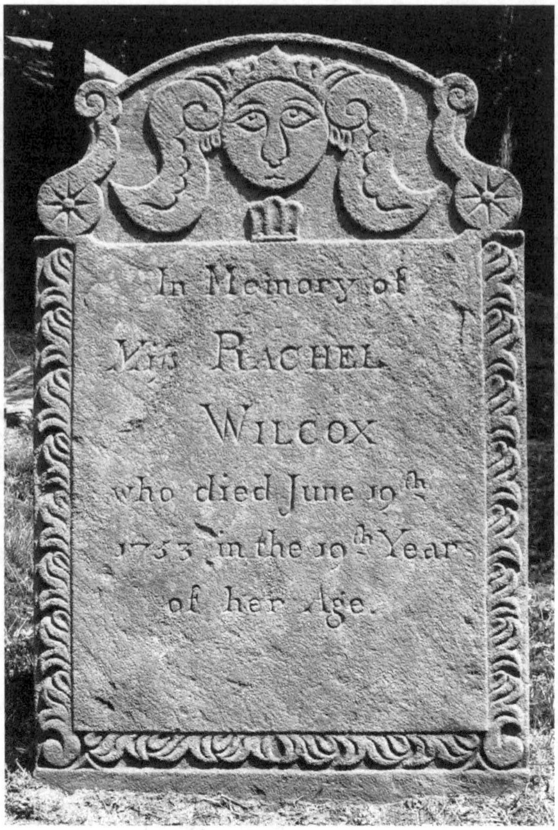

Rachel Wilcox, 1753.

Joseph Willcoks, 1747.

Samuel Towner, 1810.

Rebekah Willcoks, 1758. Gneiss, 19"w x 32"h.

Sarah Willcox, 1775.

Wellington L. Wilcox, 1852. Marble, 19"h.

Union District Cemetery.

Southwest District Cemetery. The Southwest District cemetery is the second oldest in Killingworth, having been laid out October 7, 1743. It is located on River Road just south of Green Hill Road. This cemetery is in relatively good condition and has a number of eighteenth century gravestones. There are six children of Aaron and Lydia Kelcey buried in this cemetery. Four of them died within a period of four days in 1777. The finest gravestone in Killingworth is that of Eli Kelsey. He died in 1788 just before his graduation from Yale College. His epitaph was written by Ezra Stiles, President of Yale College. The stone was carved by John Johnson. It is 69 inches high and 32 inches wide at the base and made of a durable type of sandstone.

Southwest District Cemetery.

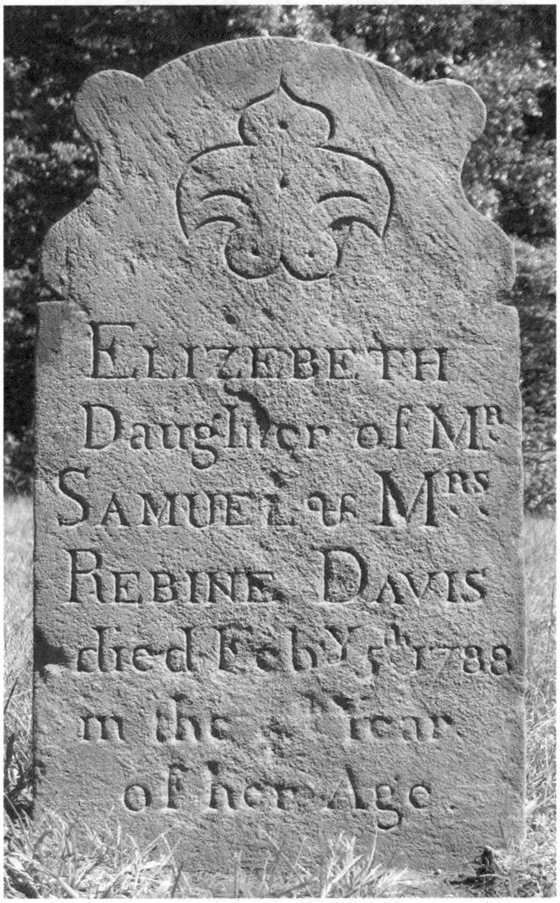

Elizebeth Davis, 1788.

Rebine Davis, 1793.

Sarah Davis, 1833.

Sibbel Dudley, 1808.

Joseph Farnham, 1801.

Jared Griswold, 1784.

Martin Griswold, 1794.

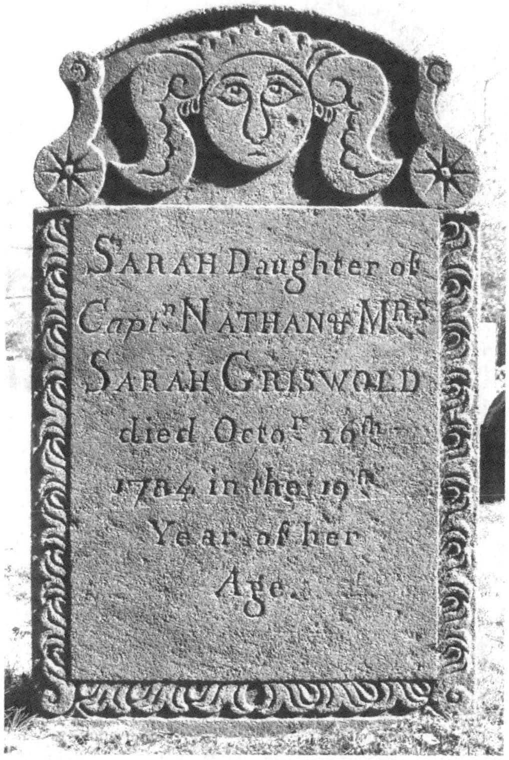

Sarah Griswold, 1784.

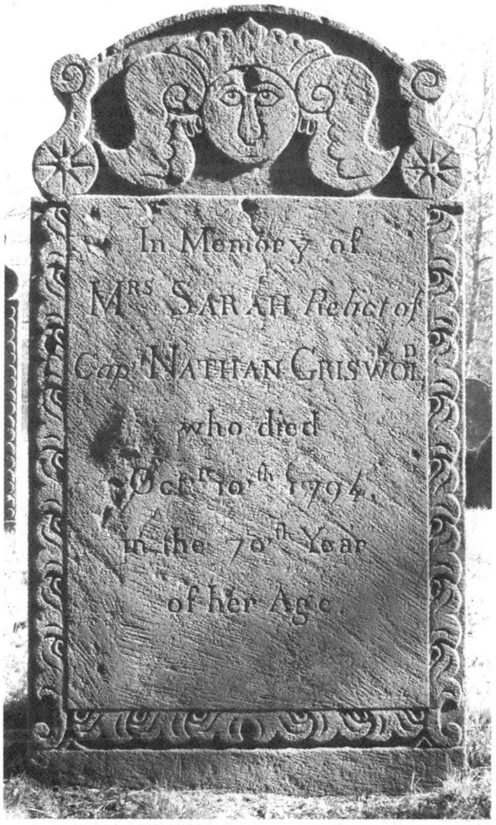

Sarah Griswold, 1794.

Elisabeth Hull, 1769.

Capt. James Hull, 1820.

Capt. Lemuel Hull, 1793.

Aaron Kelcey, 1781.

Careline Kelcey, 1777.

Chloe Kelcey, 1777.

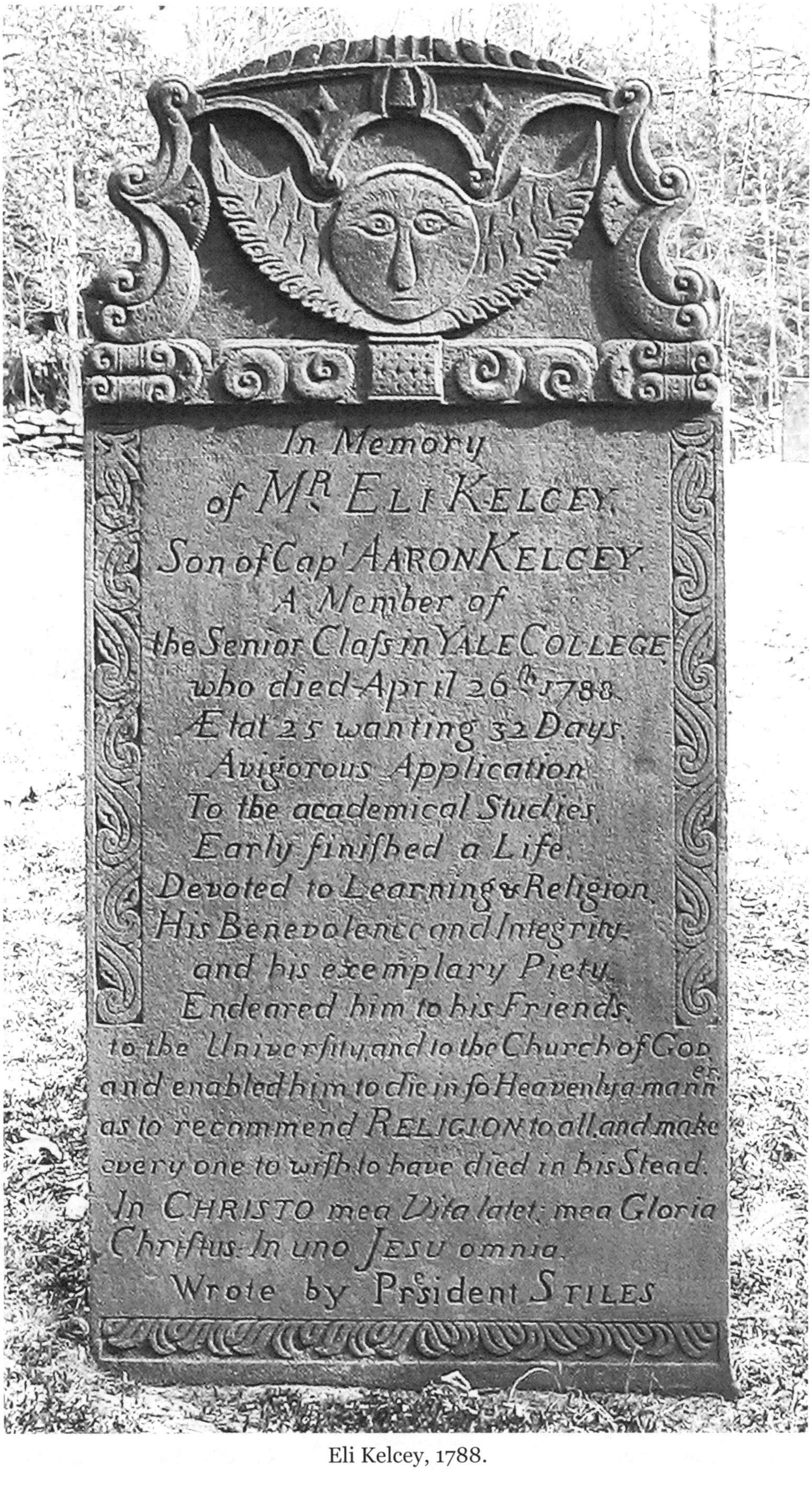

Eli Kelcey, 1788.

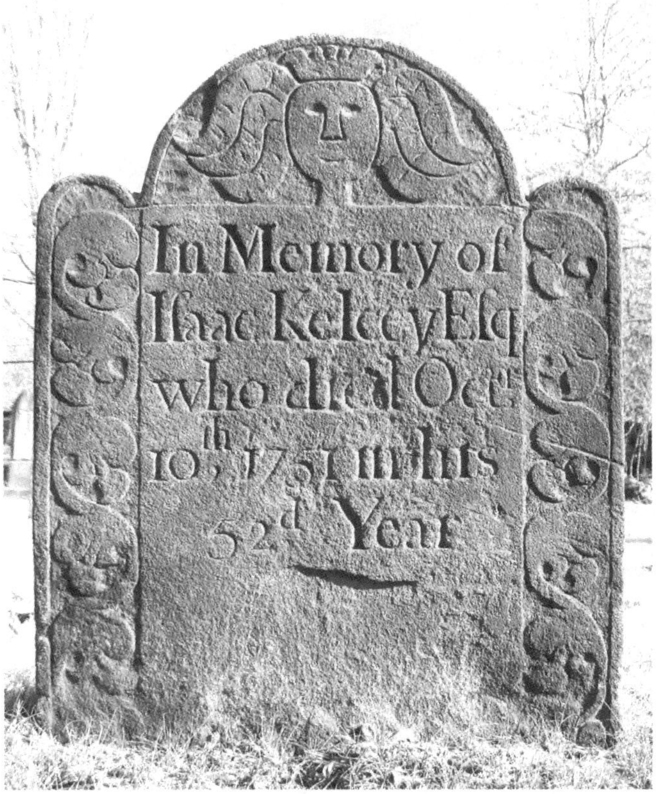

Isaac Kelcey Esq, 1776.

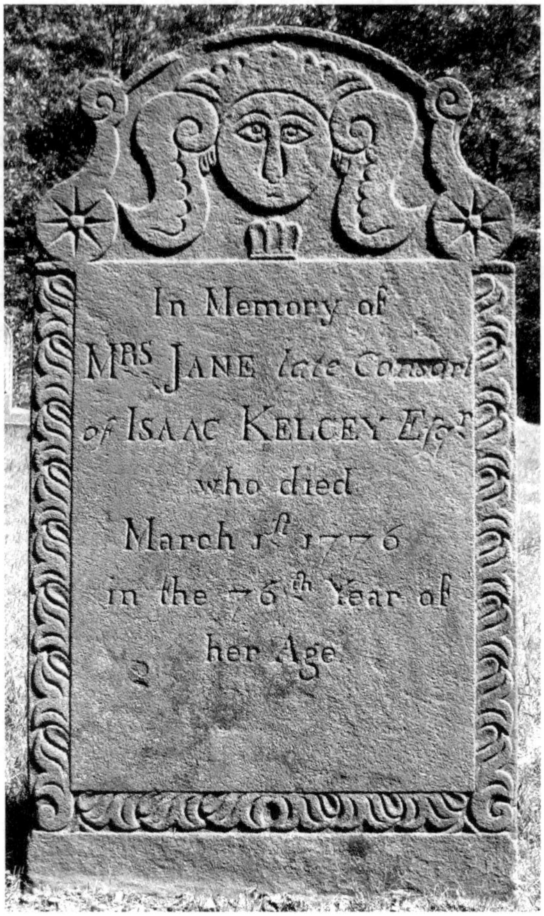

Jane Kelcey, 1776.

Jonah Kelcey, 1772.

Capt. Nathan Kelcey, 1751.

Lucy Kelsey, 1784.

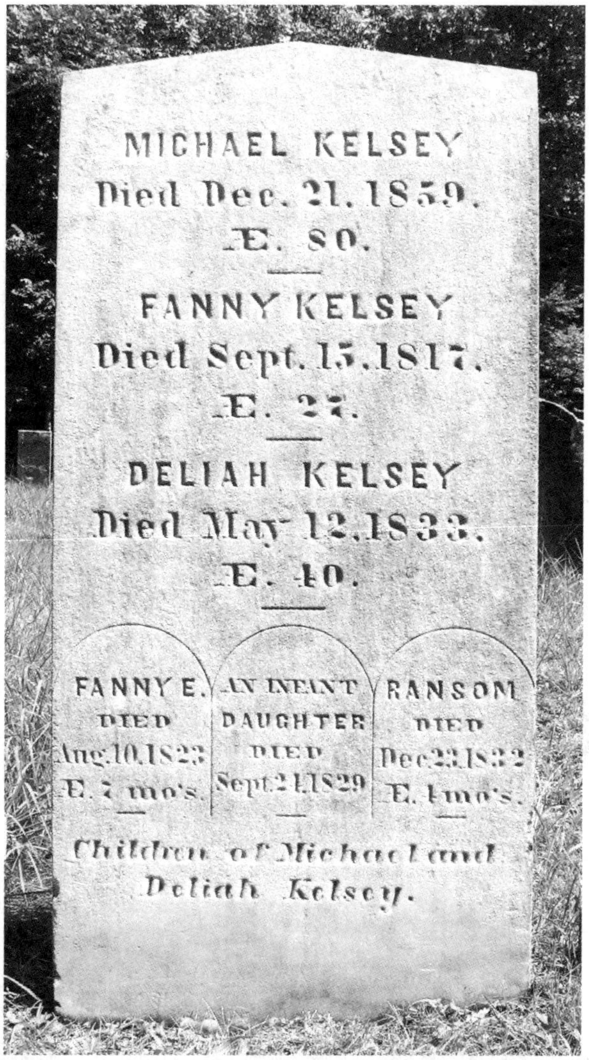

Michael Kelsey Family, 1859.

Nettleton Family plot.

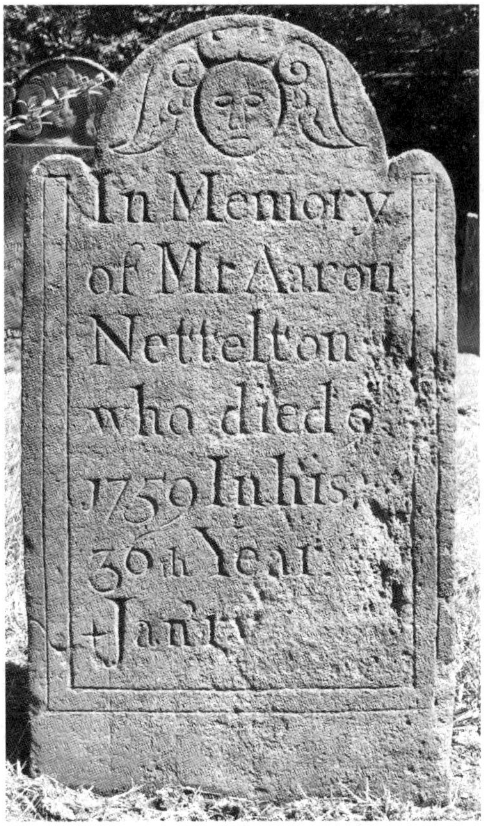

Aaron Nettelton, 1759.

Hannah Nettelton, 1753.

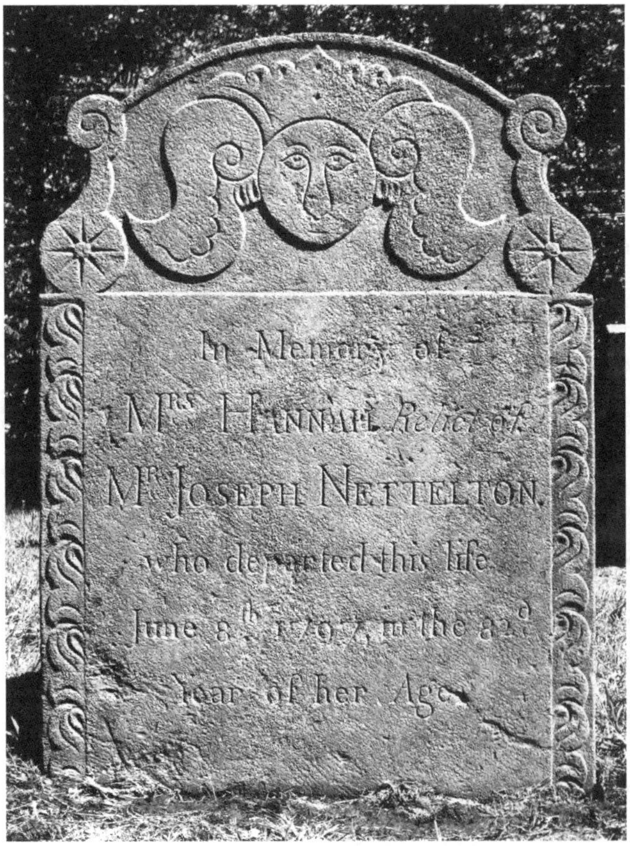

Hannah Nettelton, 1797.

Joseph Nettelton, 1767.

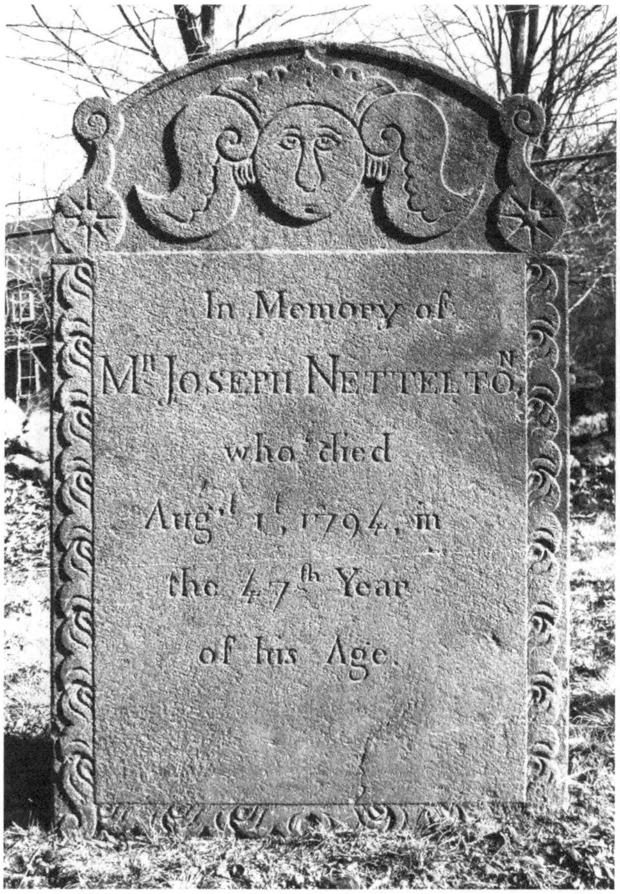

Joseph Nettelton, 1794.

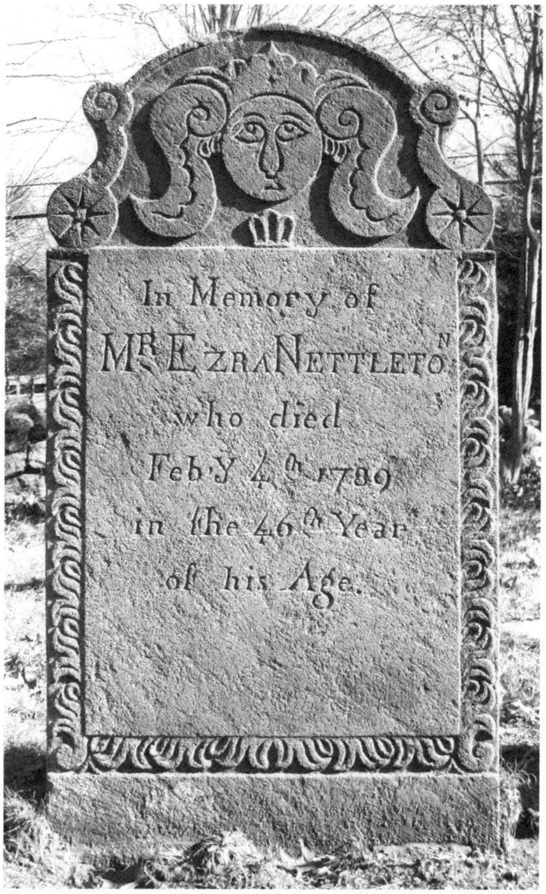

Ezra Nettleton, 1789.

John Nettlton, 1753.

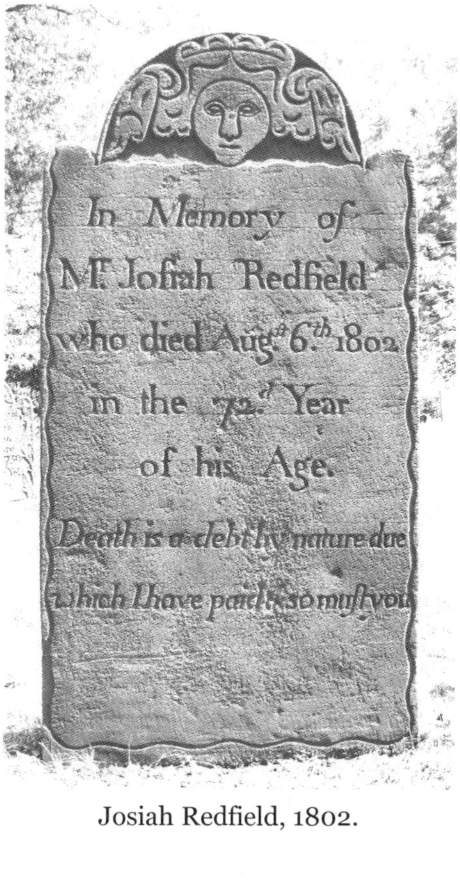

Josiah Redfield, 1802.

Diana Teall, 1756.

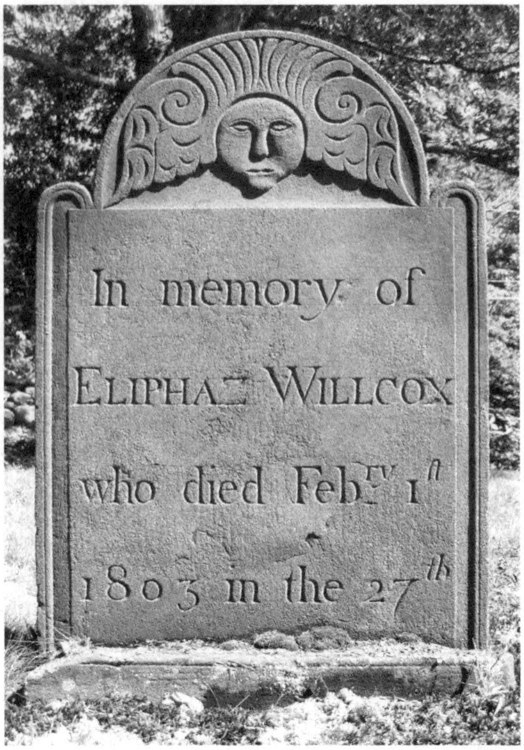

Eliphaz Willcox, 1803.

Pine Orchard District Cemetery. This burying ground located on North Chestnut Hill Road is the third oldest in Killingworth being laid out on November 7, 1748. It was called the Nettleton Cemetery before the name of the Nettleton District was changed to Pine Orchard District in the nineteenth century. It is called the Old Cemetery in the Hale Collection. A number of veterans of the French and Indian War are buried here. The cemetery was a burying ground for victims of smallpox. It was also used as a burying site for Native Americans. There are many fieldstone markers that were often used for Native Americans. A Native American named Jim Soobuck and his children are buried here. The cemetery is located in a remote area and has suffered from extensive vandalism. Teenagers often met there for parties and drinking. In May 1981, the bodies of two young men were found slumped against two headstones. Both were shot in the head and a rifle was found nearby. The deaths were considered a murder/suicide, but questions remain. In recent years, some houses have been built nearby and the vandalism has ceased, but the damage has been done. There remain only ten intact eighteenth century headstones.

Pine Orchard District Cemetery.

Fieldstone.

Mary Bacon, 1812.

Rachel Blatchly, 1795.

Bezaleel Bristol, 1753.

Eunice Bristol, 1755.

Lydia Graves, 1789.

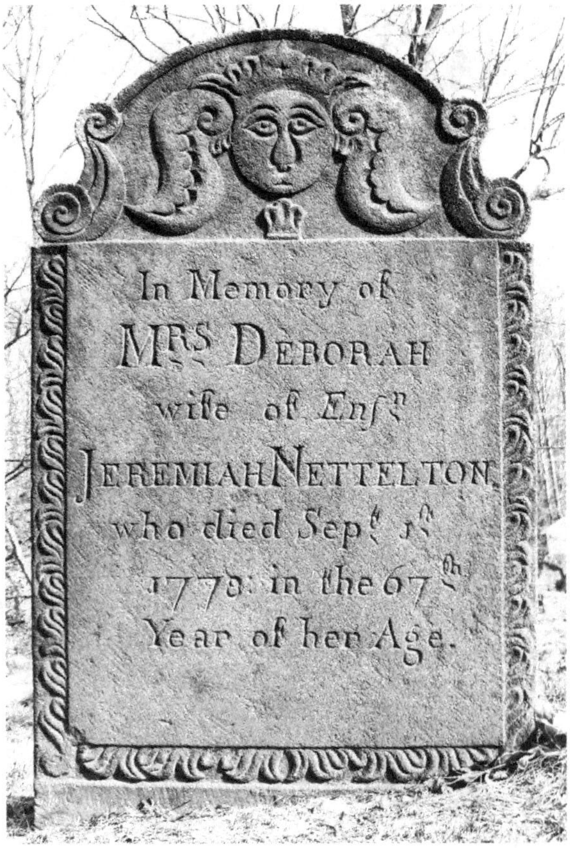

Deborah Nettelton, 1778.

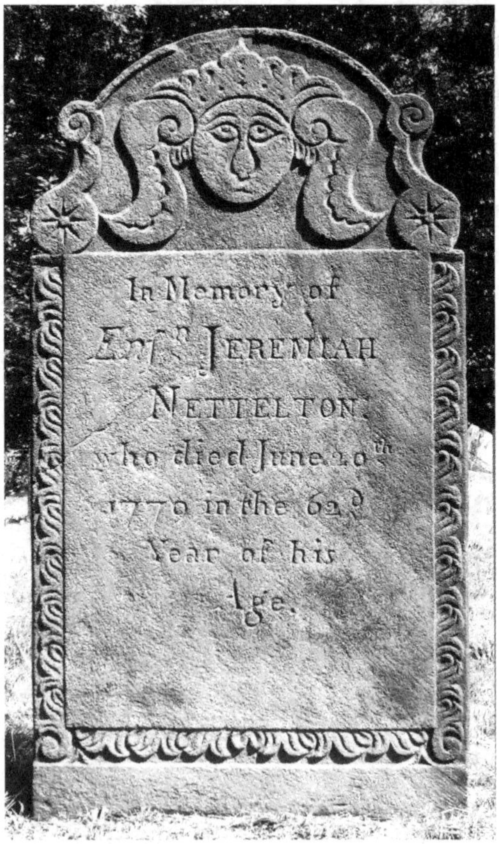

Ensn. Jeremiah Nettelton, 1779.

Lydia Nettelton, 1794.

Mary Norton, 1799.

Experience Willcoks, 1790.

Lucretia Willcox, 1777.

Stone House District Cemetery. The Stone House District Cemetery is located on Little City Road a short distance north of Route 148. It was established on May 5, 1806.

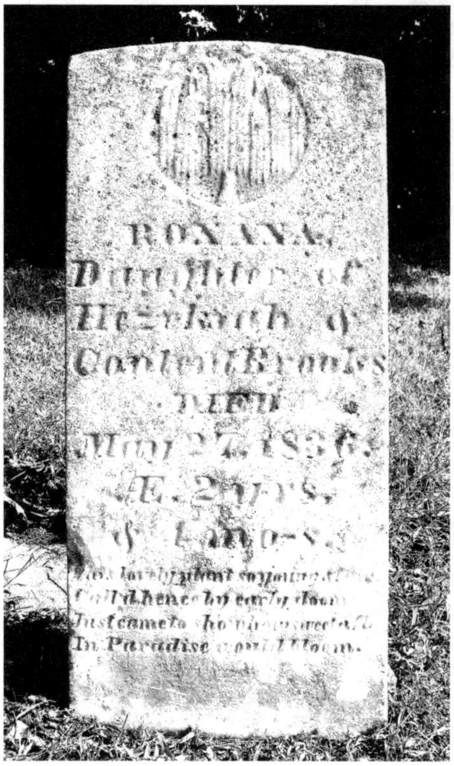

Roxana Brooks, 1836.

Freeborn G. Burr, 1803.

Israel W. Burr, 1845.

David Evarts, 1826.

Hannah Evarts, 1803.

Esther Nettleton, 1813.

Lane District Cemetery. This cemetery is located on Lovers Lane. It was established in 1835 although there is a marker dated 1830. Although called the Lane District Cemetery, earlier Lanes are buried in the Union District Cemetery and many later Lanes are in the Parker Hill District Cemetery. The cemetery was used as a "potters field" into the twentieth century for burial of the indigent. There are many unmarked graves in this cemetery.

Part of Lane District Cemetery.

Jonathan Kelsey, 1835.

Joseph Lane, 1844.

Emily M. Lane, 1855, and Infant Son, 1844.

Parker Hill District Cemetery. This cemetery is located on North Parker Hill Road. It is mistakenly called the Nettleton Cemetery in the Hale Collection. It was established on October 16, 1837, although the oldest gravestone is dated 1835. This cemetery is said to be haunted. The ghosts of a bride and groom have been reported to cross the road both to and from the cemetery. Other strange phenomena are said to have been seen and experienced in this cemetery.

Mary J. Burr, 1876.

Willie Burr, 1873.

John, 1893, and Almira, 1901, Griswold.

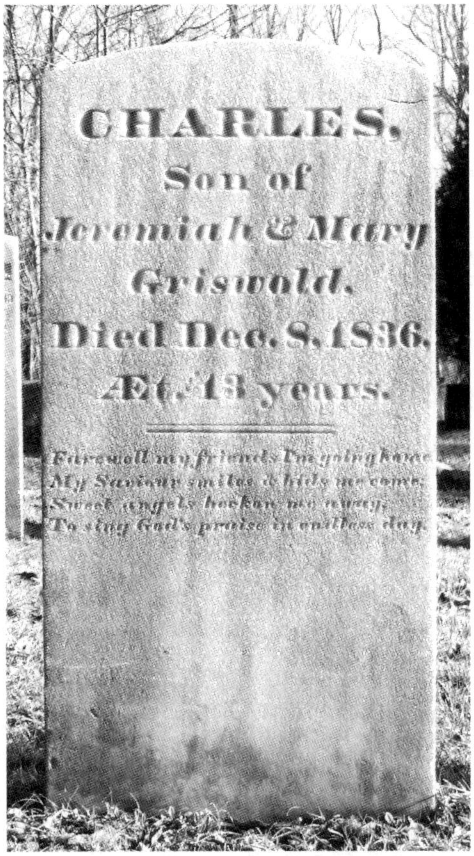

Charles Griswold, 1836.

Philander H., 1837, and Calvin H., 1848, Hull.

Philetta Hull, 1871.

Charles D., 1890, and Olive Stone, 1876, Kelsey.

Ronald Kelsey, 1893.

Elsietta A. Lane, 1854.

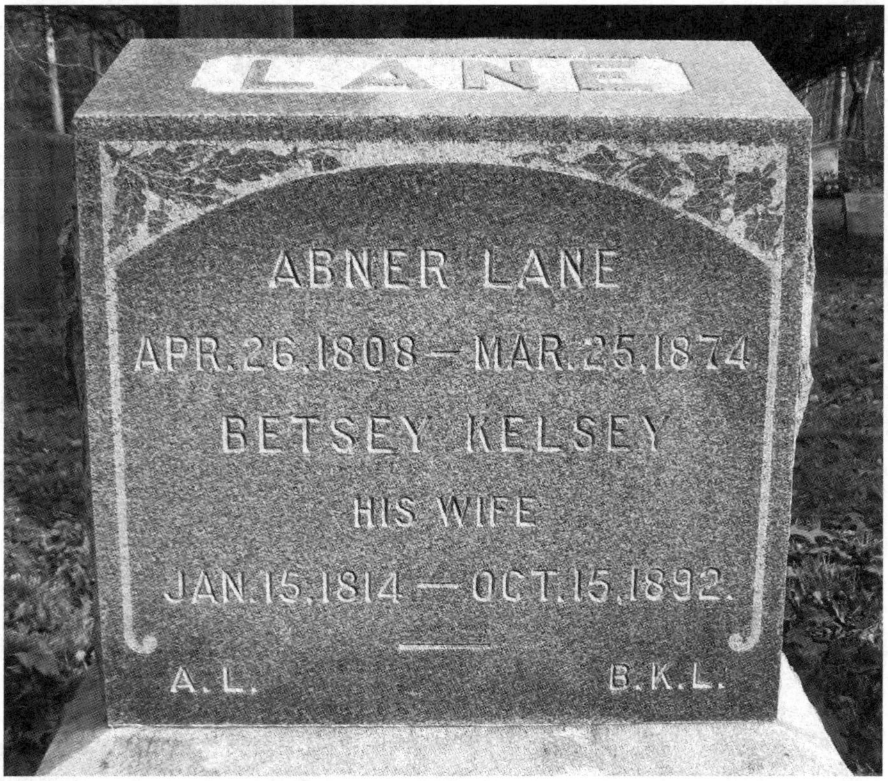

Abner Lane, 1874, and Betsey Kelsey Lane, 1892.

Abner Lane was a prominent inventor and scientist. He was one of the pioneers and leading manufacturers of axe helves and pick axe handles and invented a machine for this purpose. He operated two axe handle manufactories in Killingworth.

Gideon Lane, 1873.

Jeremiah K., 1891, and Mary Eliza, 1893, Lane.

Alexander A. Newlands, 1883.

Nathan, 1892, and Betsey M., 1894, Lane.

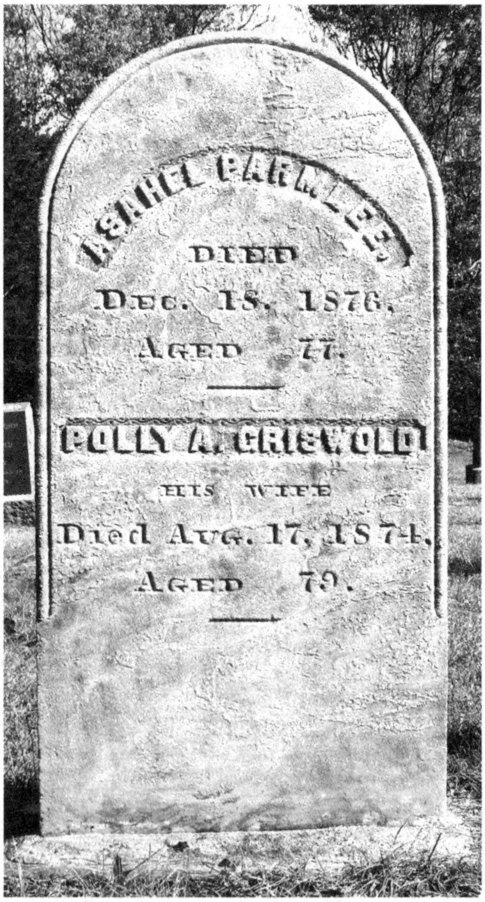

Asahel, 1876, and Polly Griswold, 1874, Parmelee.

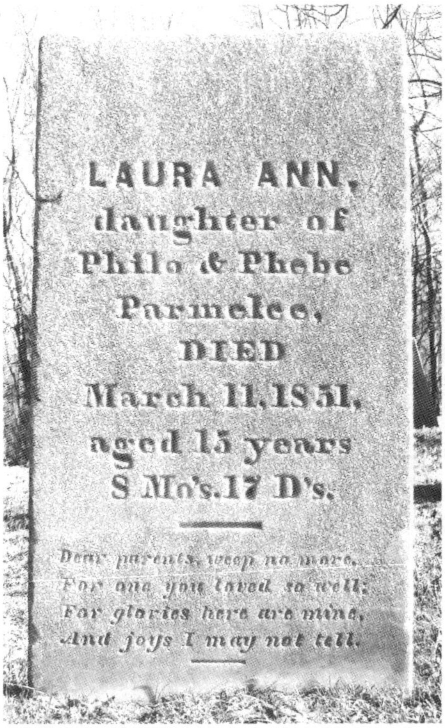

Laura Ann Parmelee, 1851.

Ezra Rutty, 1852.

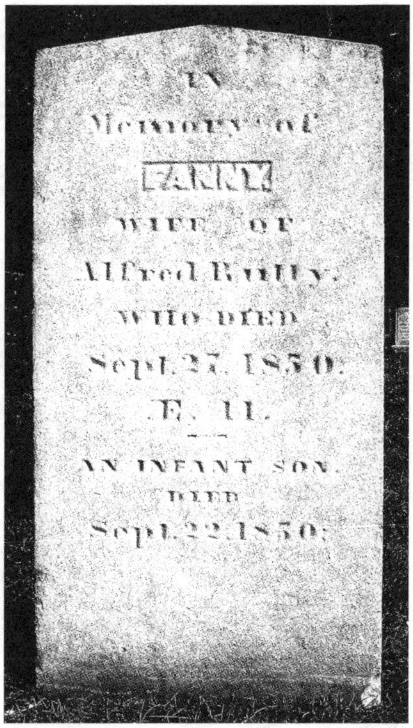

Fanny Rutty and an Infant Son, 1850.

New Pine Orchard District (Emmanuel Church) Cemetery. This cemetery is located on Bunnell Bridge Road in a very remote and undeveloped area. It was established in 1875 on land donated by the Bristol family, long-standing members of Emmanuel Episcopal Church. It was known as the Emmanuel Church Cemetery. The cemetery was transferred from the church to the Town of Killingworth in 1948 and is now called the New Pine Orchard District Cemetery. It is closed except to existing plot owners. There are a number of unmarked burials in the cemetery.

Samuel A. Bunnell, 1887.

Dudley Family, 1879–1923.

William Kelsey and Sarah M. Munger Kelsey, 1894.

Christina Fuerstenberg, 1907.

Evergreen Cemetery. The Evergreen Cemetery is located on both sides of Green Hill Road and was established in 1856 and incorporated in 1863. The earliest stone is dated 1834. It is privately owned and well maintained by the Evergreen Cemetery Association. In 1915, the Association acquired land on the southeast side of Green Hill Road. This section of the Evergreen Cemetery is erroneously called the New Southwest District Cemetery in the Hale Collection. The Evarts Family monument is located in this section of the cemetery. In 1954-1955, the Mary S. McAtee Memorial Wall was built along Green Hill Road in memory of her parents Hosmer E. and Elizabeth H. Stevens. The Evergreen Cemetery is the only active cemetery in Killingworth.

Evarts Family, 1915–1946.

Henry Chittenden, 1892. Monumental Bronze Co.

Rachel C. Evarts, 1876.

Hugh Lofting, 1947.

Anna L. [Griswold], 1874.

Hugh John Lofting created the character of Doctor Dolittle, one of the classics of children's literature. He lived across from the cemetery.

Minnie E. and Nellie F. [Griswold], 1871.

Herman, 1953, and Bertha, 1964, Heser.

Clarence A. Parmelee, 1877.

Elwood D. Parmelee, 1844.

Horace L., 1898, and Eunice M. Parmelee, 1905.

Daniel Stevens, 1879.

Washington A., 1904, and Cynthia M. Snow, 1909.

Randolph P. Stevens Family, 1850–1898.

Gravestones of the Clergy

In Colonial times, the pastors of the Congregational Church were the most important and influential members of the community. Communities went to great lengths and expense to obtain a suitable pastor. The pastor, though, also had to maintain peace and harmony in the congregation, sometimes a difficult undertaking especially during periods of religious dissension. Many pastors resigned or were dismissed and moved to other towns and it was rare for a pastor to spend his entire lifetime in one congregation. There are three early pastors whose remains reside in Killingworth; Abraham Pierson, Jared Eliot, and William Seward. These are among the most important people in the history of Killingworth.

In 1663, the General Assembly of the Colony of Connecticut drew up regulations for the ordering of the Plantation of "Homonoscitt." Among the provisions in October 1663 was "That they Shall Settle an able orthodoxe godly Minister free from Scandall, with the advise of the major part of the Magistrates & ministirs in Connecticott." The Rev. John Cotton (1640–1699), a Harvard graduate and son of John Cotton of Massachusetts, is said to have first ministered to the spiritual needs of the community (Thoms, 1967). John Cotton was the pastor in Wethersfield at the time. In 1667, he became the pastor in Plymouth, Massachusetts.

Gravestone of Warham Mather (1666–1745) in the crypt of the First Church of Christ in New Haven.

The Rev. John Woodbridge (1644–1691) of Andover, Massachusetts who first preached in the new settlement in 1666 was called to be the first pastor in 1667. Mr. Woodbridge was born in 1644 and graduated from Harvard College in 1664 at age 20. He was ordained in Killingworth on April 7, 1669. In 1671, he married Abigail Leete, with whom he had six children. She was a daughter of William Leete (c1613–1683), Governor of the New Haven Colony and later the Connecticut Colony. Mr. Woodbridge was pastor until 1678/9 when he resigned and became the pastor in Wethersfield where he remained until his death in 1691.

Two ministers supplied the pulpit between 1679 and 1693. James Bayley (Bailey) preached from 1682 to 1691. James Bayley (1650–1707) graduated from Harvard in 1669. He was the first pastor in Salem Village, now Danvers, Massachusetts, from 1671 to 1680 before the witch trials there. In Killingworth, a daughter aged 10, died in 1683. Another daughter, Sarah, was born on September 3, 1683, but lived only 22 days. A son, Joshua, was born in 1685. His wife, Mary, died in 1688. After his stay in Killingworth, he left the ministry and set up practice as a physician in Roxbury, Massachusetts where he is buried.

Warham Mather occupied the pulpit from 1691 to 1693. Mather (1666–1745) was a member of the influential Mather family of Puritan ministers. He graduated from Harvard in 1685 and served briefly as pastor in Northfield, Massachusetts before coming to Killingworth. Mr. Mather then removed to New Haven and entered the legal profession. He was appointed by the General Assembly as Justice of the Peace and Quorum in 1710 and also as Judge of the Court of Probate in New Haven in 1717. He is buried in the crypt under the First Church of Christ in New Haven (Center Church on-the-Green).

The Rev. Abraham Pierson (1646–1707) was called as pastor in 1694. Mr. Pierson was the son of the Rev. Abraham Pierson (c1613–1678) and Abigail Mitchell and assisted his father in the ministry in Southampton, Long Island, Branford, Connecticut, and Newark, New Jersey. Abraham Pierson, Jr. graduated from Harvard College in 1668. He was ordained on May 4, 1672, in Newark. On the death of his father in 1678, he became the pastor in Newark and was dismissed in 1692. He married Abigail Clarke (1654–1727) in 1673 and together they had nine children. The Rev. Pierson fell sick and died on March 5, 1707. His gravestone was broken off and stolen in 1936 but was recovered. It has since been removed from the Indian River Cemetery and preserved by the Clinton Historical Society.

Gravestone of the Rev. Abraham Pierson when it stood in the Killingworth Yard. 1969.

Footstone of the Rev. Abraham Pierson.

The Rev. Jared Eliot (1685–1763).

Abigail Pierson (1654–1727).

The Rev. Abraham Pierson, on his deathbed, advised those present to select Mr. Jared Eliot, one of his students, as his successor as pastor. The Rev. Jared Eliot (1685–1763) graduated from the Collegiate School in 1706. He began ministerial duties on June 1, 1707, but was not ordained until October 26, 1709. Mr. Eliot was called to be pastor at a town meeting held on November 5, 1708.

Jared Eliot was born in 1685. His paternal grandfather was John Eliot (1604–1690), the celebrated apostle to the Indians of New England. His maternal grandfather was Samuel Wyllys (1632–1709), the son of George Wyllys (c1589–1645) the second governor of the Connecticut Colony. Samuel married Ruth Haynes (1631–1688), daughter of the first governor, John Haynes (1594–1654). His father was the Rev. Joseph Eliot (1638–1694) who graduated from Harvard College in 1658 and was the pastor in Guilford, Connecticut. His mother was Mary Haynes Wyllys (1656–1729). Jared married Hannah Smithson (1693–1761) of Guilford in 1710 and they had 11 children. He served as minister for 56 years and was, in addition, a distinguished physician and scientist.

The graves of Jared Eliot and his son Aaron are marked by table tombs. A plaque was placed on Jared's tomb in 1958 by the Yale University Library. Hannah Eliot's grave is next to Jared's and is marked by a fine headstone with a soul effigy. The grave of Elizabeth, a daughter of Hannah and Jared is nearby. This interesting little stone is 15 inches high, 14 inches wide at the top and 12 ½ inches wide at the bottom. It is slate and was carved by John Stevens I (1646–1736) of Newport, Rhode Island. It has a crude winged death's head with hanging teeth at the top.

Nathaniel Chauncey was the pastor in Durham from 1706 to 1756. He studied under Abraham Pierson in Killingworth and received his degree at the first commencement of the Collegiate School in 1702.

The table tomb on the right is that of the Rev. Jared Eliot (1685–1763) and the one on the left is that of Jared's son Aaron (1718–1785). Indian River Cemetery.

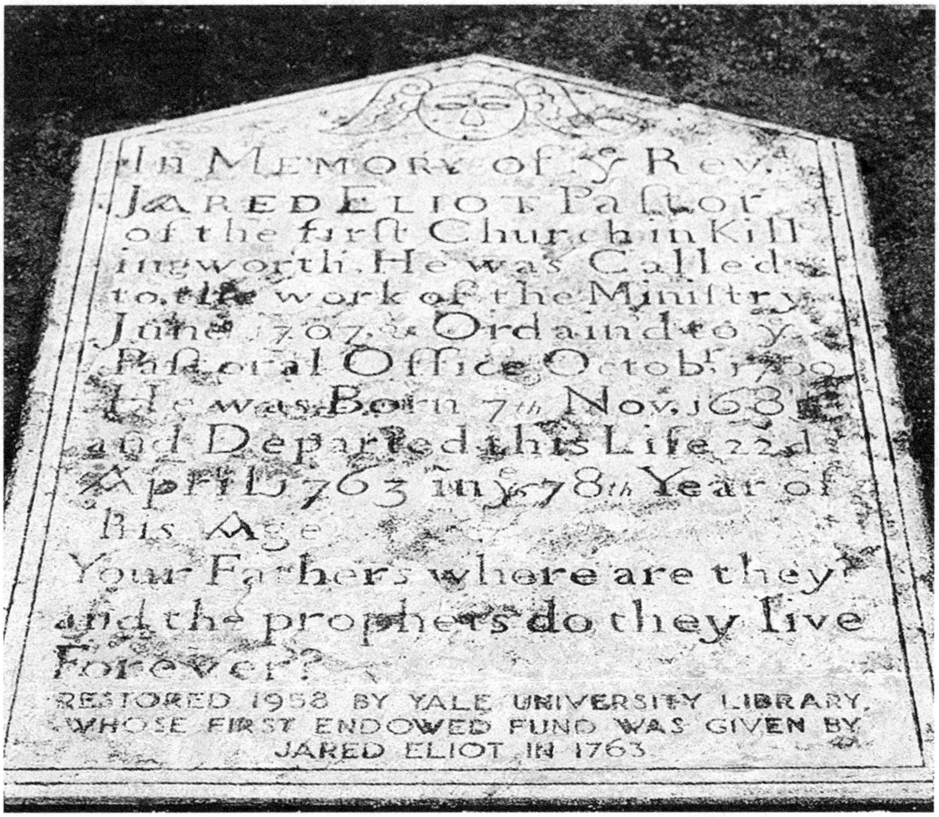

Plaque on top of Jared Eliot tomb, now deteriorated.

Hannah Eliot (1693–1761), wife of Jared. Sandstone, 30"w x 48"h. Indian River Cemetery.

Elizabeth Eliot (1711–1713), daughter of Jared and Hannah Eliot. Indian River Cemetery.

Mary Wyllys Eliot (1656–1729), wife of the Rev. Joseph Eliot, the pastor in Guilford, and mother of Jared Eliot. Indian River Cemetery.

Chest tomb of Nathaniel Chauncey (1681-1756) and Sarah Chauncey (1683-1745). Old Durham Cemetery.

The Reverend William Seward (1712–1782), first pastor of the Second Church of Christ in Killingworth. Painting c1750.

The Rev. William Seward, also called Seaward, was the first pastor in the Second Ecclesiastical Society, now present Killingworth. He was born in Durham, July 27, 1712. William Seward's great-grandfather was William Seward of Guilford (1627–1689) who married Grace Norton (1632–1702). William Seward of Guilford was Lieutenant of the Train Band and represented Guilford as Deputy to the General Court in 1673, 1674, 1683, 1684, and 1685. The Rev. William Seward's grandfather was Capt. John Seward (1654–1748) of Guilford and Durham, who married Abigail Bushnell. Capt. John Seward was one of the founders of Durham and served as Deputy to the General Court in 1704, 1705, 1708, and 1709. William Seward's father was Deacon William Seward (1683/4–1764) of Durham, Guilford, and Killingworth who married Damaris Punderson (1680–1740). He moved to Killingworth to be with his son and is buried in the Union District Cemetery. Mr. Seward received his degree of Bachelor of Arts from Yale College in 1734 and received a masters degree in 1737. He was called to be pastor in 1737. The ordination of Mr. Seward took place in the church in the First Society on January 18, 1738. This is the date usually given for the formation of the Second Congregational Church. Mr. Seward was 25 at the time he became Pastor in North Killingworth. His ministry in Killingworth lasted 44 years until his death in 1782 at the age of 70. His ministry and that of Jared Eliot are among the longest in a single church in New England.

The Rev. William Seward of Killingworth was married three times. Members of the Rev. Seward's family; his father, two wives Concurrence and Mabel, and some of his children are buried in the Union District Cemetery. His own gravestone was removed from the cemetery and placed in the Congregational church when it began to deteriorate. There are markers for two infants, John who died in 1750 aged 17 days and a second John who died in 1763 aged one year and 12 days. Mabel probably died from complications of childbirth as she died about two months after giving birth to a stillborn son in 1768. John Punderson Seward was the younger son of the Rev. Seward. He came home to Killingworth from Yale to have his graduation suit of homespun made in 1784 and died suddenly of scarlet fever at the age of 19. His gravestone is one of the most impressive in Killingworth. There are many such instances of young men in college dying of diseases for which there was no treatment, probably because living in an urban area increased their exposure to contagious diseases. William Seward was the only pastor to live and die in present Killingworth. A daughter of the Rev. Hiram Bell who was pastor from 1850 to 1864 is buried in the Union District Cemetery.

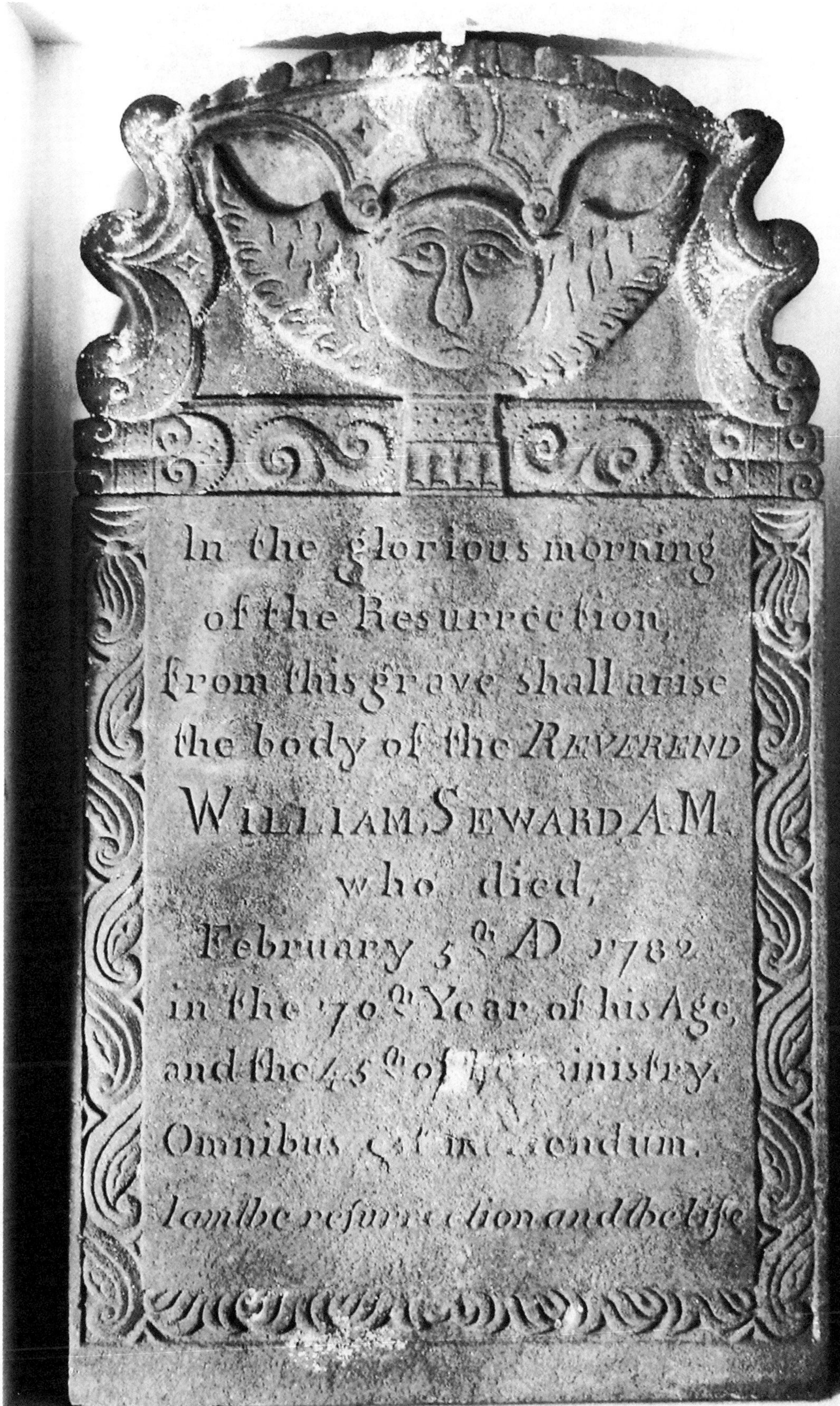

Gravestone of the Rev. William Seward (1712–1782) in the Congregational Church.

Deacon William Seaward (1683/4–1764), father of the Rev. William Seward. Union District Cemetery.

John Seward (1682–1748), uncle of the Rev. William Seward. Sandstone, 20"w x 27"h, Old Durham Cemetery.

Concurrence Seaward (1709–1753), first wife of the Rev. William Seward. Sandstone, 24”w x 46”h.

Mabel Seaward, 1768, second wife of the Rev. William Seward. Red sandstone, 23 ½"w x 42" h.

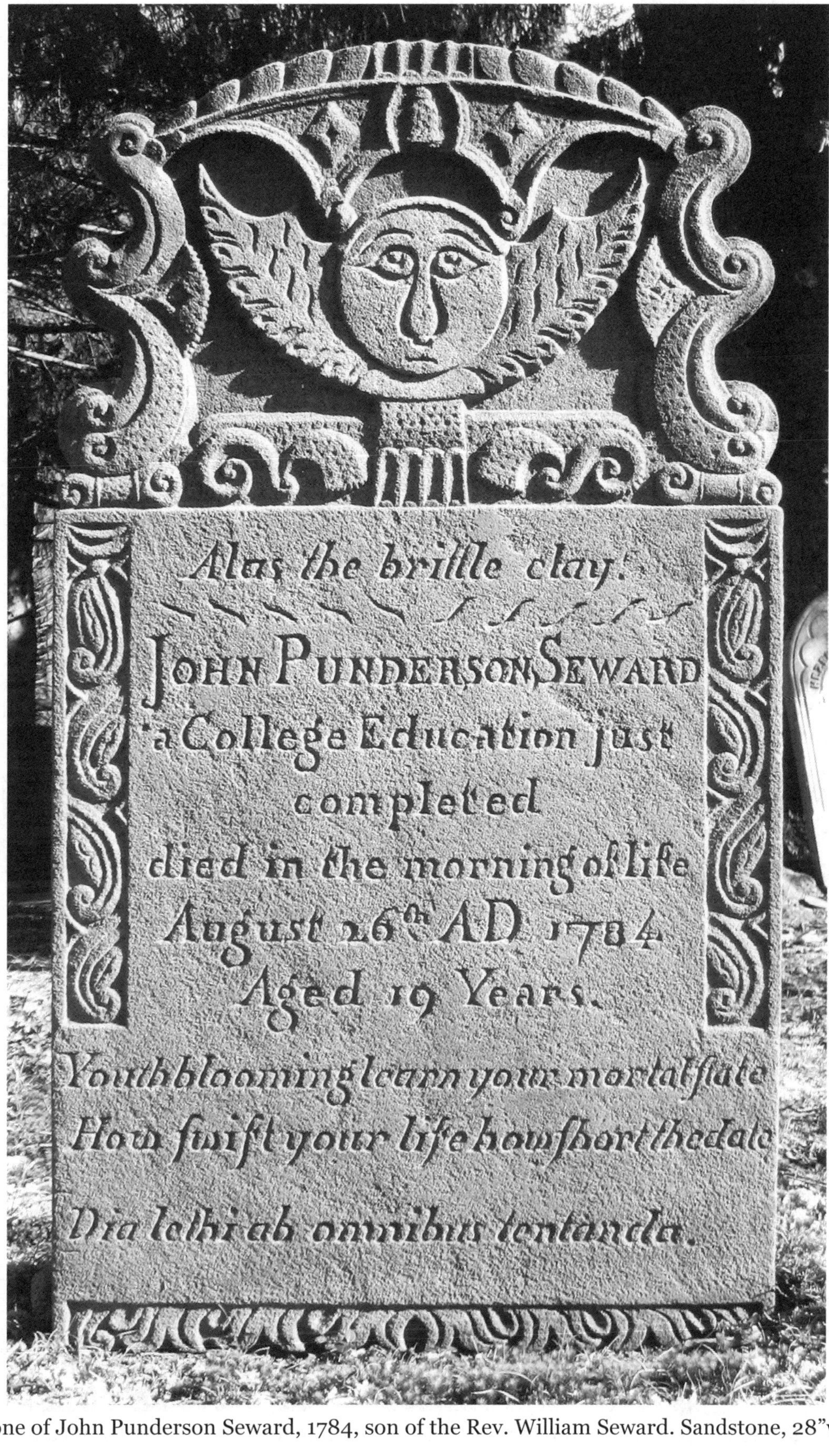

Gravestone of John Punderson Seward, 1784, son of the Rev. William Seward. Sandstone, 28"w x 50"h.

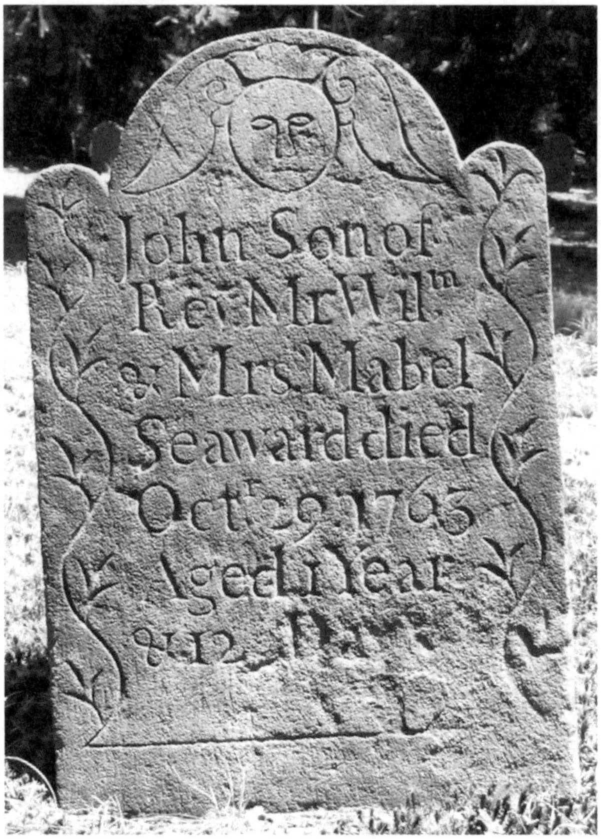

Gravestones of two young sons of Mr. Seward. John, son of William and Concurrence Seaward, his first wife, and John, son of William and Mabel Seaward, his second wife.

Stillborn son of the Rev. William and Mabel Seaward.

Daughter of the Rev. Hiram and Mary Bell.

Gravestones of the Deacons

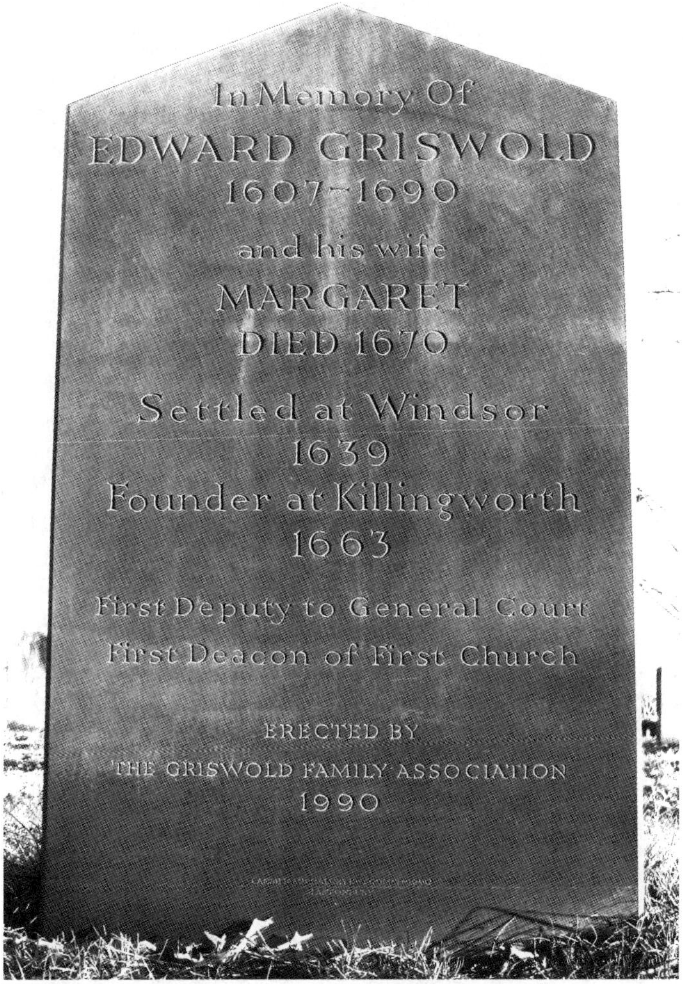

Memorial for Edward and Margaret Griswold.

The gravestones that could be found of the early deacons are illustrated in this chapter. The deacons were highly respected in the community in colonial times. Prior to the formation of the Second Society, the deacons were Edward Griswold, Henry Farnam, John Griswold, Nathaniel Parmelee, John Lane, Josiah Stevens, and Josiah Hull. Edward Griswold (1607–1690) was the first deacon and the most significant person in the founding of the town. He lived in Kenilworth, Warwickshire, England and married Margaret Hicks (1610–1670) in 1630. They had 11 children in England and Windsor, Connecticut. Edward, his wife, and young children came to America and settled in Dorcester, Massachusetts. In 1649, he moved a few miles out of Windsor up the Farmington River to Poquonock. He was active in the affairs of the town and colony and served as Deputy to the General Court for Windsor, justice of the peace, on trials of persons accused of witchcraft, and built the Old Fort at Springfield. In 1663 Edward and his son John removed from Poquonock to Hammonasset. It is surprising that someone his age would leave an established homestead to essentially start over again in a new wilderness. At this time, there was ecclesiastical strife in New England churches over the halfway covenant, and Edward may have moved to avoid the dissension in the Windsor church. He arrived at a new settlement at the age of 56 already having accomplished much in his life. He immediately took a leadership role in the new plantation and was a petitioner to the General Court for the establishment of a new church and was the first deacon. Since he came from Kenilworth, Warwickshire, England, he was probably instrumental in having the name changed by the General Court to Kenilworth in 1667. He then served for 22 more years as Deputy for Kenilworth to the General Court. After the death of Margaret in 1670, he married the widow Sarah Bemis in 1672. Genealogies give his death in the 84th year of his age on August 30, but differ as to whether it was in 1690 or 1691. There is no stone marking his burial in the Indian River Cemetery. A fine memorial was erected by the Griswold Family Association in 1990. A slab of rough gneiss marked "MG 1670" marks his wife Margaret's grave. Of the first deacons, the gravestones of John Griswould, John Lane, and Josiah Steevens are in the Indian River Cemetery. John Lane was also a Deputy to the General Assembly and Justice of the Peace for the county of New London. Josiah Hull moved to North Killingworth and is buried in the Southwest District Cemetery.

Deacon John Griswould, 1717.

Deacon John Lane, 1759.

Deacon Josiah Steevens, 1754.

Deacon Josiah Hull, 1759.

Joseph Willcoks was the first deacon in the Second Society beginning with the establishment of the church in 1738. Daniel Buell was appointed in 1759. Both were original settlers in North Killingworth. Dodo Pierson, the third deacon, and his son Abraham, the fifth deacon, served in the Revolutionary War. The fourth deacon, Abel Wilcox, was a town selectman and also a Revolutionary War soldier.

The First Deacons in the Second Society of Killingworth

Joseph Willcoks	1738–1774	Abel Wilcox	1831–1877
Daniel Buel	1759–1782	Heman S. Franklin	1841–1850
Dodo Pierson	1768–1796	Jared Rutty	1842–1863
Abel Wilcox	1773–1807	Julius Buell	1854–1885
Abraham Pierson	1794–1823	Lauren L. Nettleton	1854–1910
John Hinckley	1806–1849	Sherman E. Griswold	1885–1919
Nathan Hull	1814–1831	Norman L. Parmelee	1885–1923

Headstone and footstone of Joseph Willcoks (1695/6–1774), first Deacon. Union District Cemetery.

Headstone and footstone of Daniel Buel (1698–1782), second Deacon. Union District Cemetery.

Dodo Pierson, was the third deacon of the Congregational Church from 1768 to 1796. He was the grandson of Abraham Pierson, pastor of the First Church. Dodo's son, Abraham, was the fifth deacon from 1794 to 1823. Both Dodo and Abraham served in the Revolutionary War. Abraham was born on August 11, 1756 and was extensively involved in public life. In 1780, he was chosen lister (assessor) for the town, was selectman in 1781, town clerk from 1786 to 1814, captain of the militia in 1786, representative to the General Assembly for 24 sessions from 1788 to 1819, and justice of the peace from 1786 to 1814. He died May 11, 1823. His son, Dr. William S. Pierson, was a practicing physician in Windsor and was for many years president of the State Medical Society. He died July 16, 1860 leaving one son, General William S. Pierson of Windsor, who donated the organ to the Congregational Church in 1875.

The gravestone of Abraham Pierson is of special significance because it lists five generations of the Pierson family. It begins with the Rev. Abraham Pierson (c1609–1678) who was a strong Puritan. He came from England in 1640 and founded Southampton, Long Island. In 1647, he moved to Branford, Connecticut and founded the church there. Rev. Pierson published an "Indian Catechism" for the Quinnipiac Indians in 1658. He was a strict Congregationalist and refused to accept the annexation of the New Haven Colony by the Connecticut Colony where persons other than Congregationalists could vote. In 1667, he, along with most of his congregation, emigrated to New Jersey and founded as a theocracy the village of Newark. The genealogy continues with the Rev. Abraham Pierson, Abraham Pierson, Esqr., and Dea. Dodo Pierson. Unfortunately the stone was broken. Half of it was found leaning against another gravestone and the other half was buried. It has since been restored and reset.

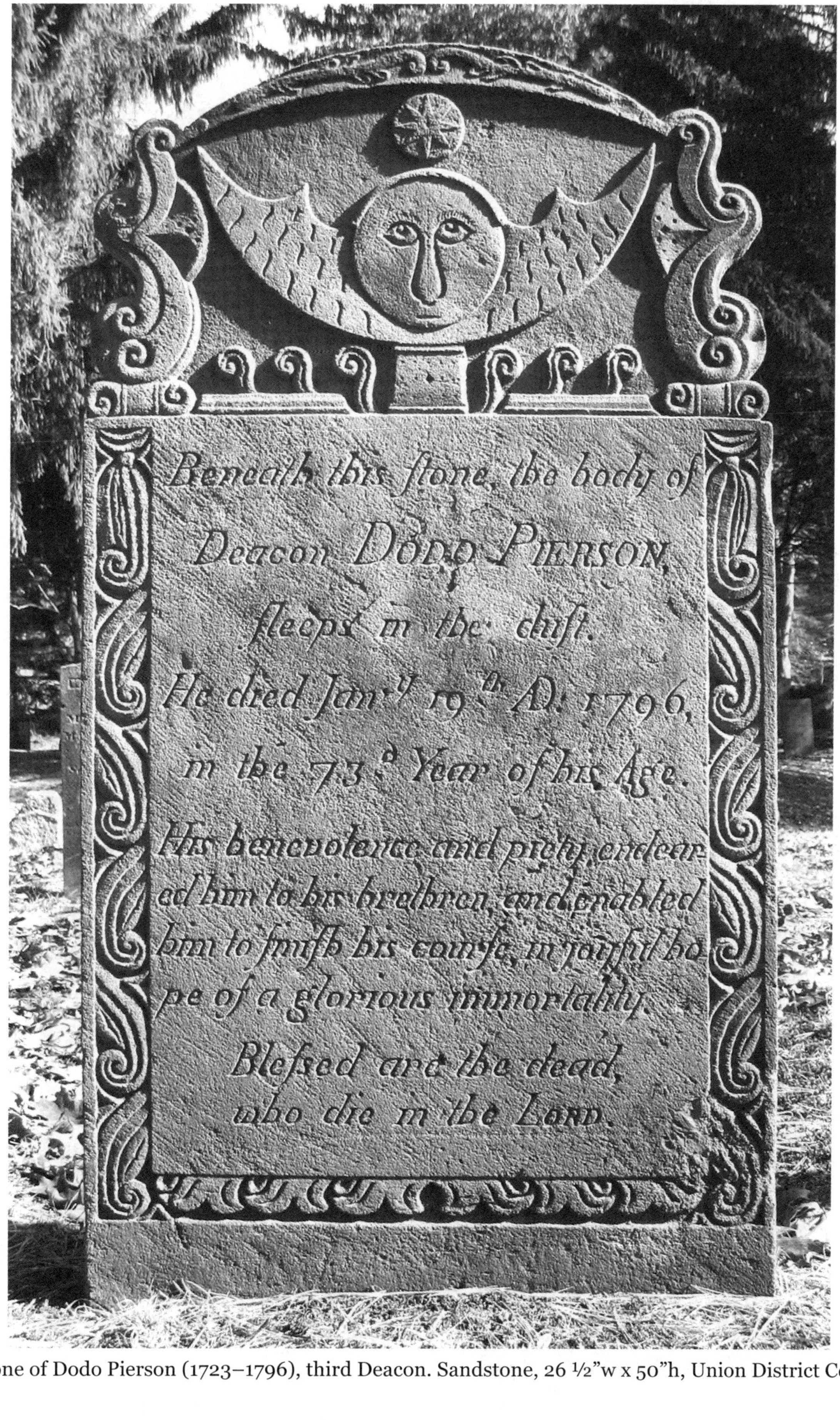

Gravestone of Dodo Pierson (1723–1796), third Deacon. Sandstone, 26 ½"w x 50"h, Union District Cemetery.

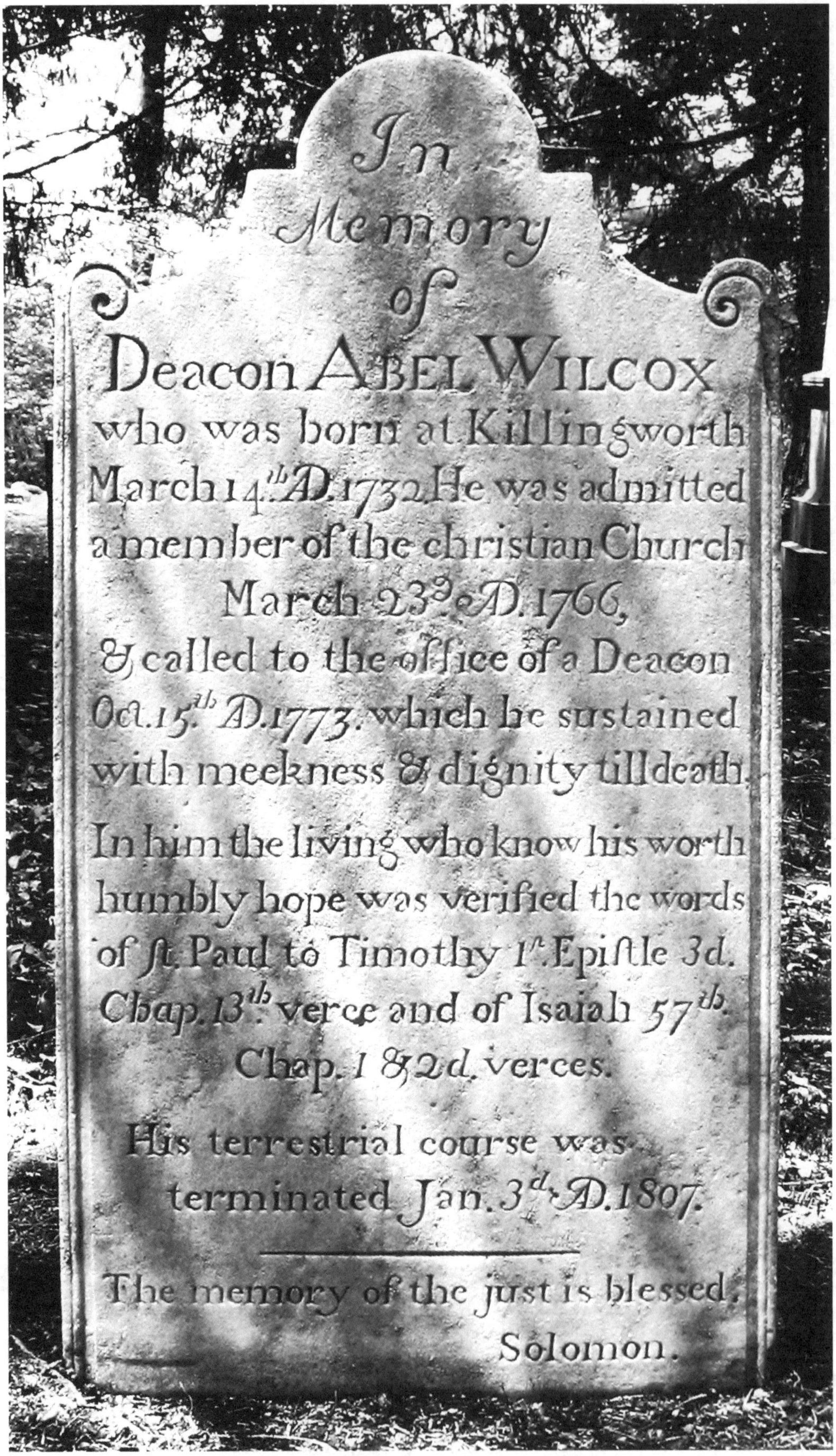

Memorial stone of Abel Wilcox (1732–1807), fourth Deacon. Union District Cemetery.

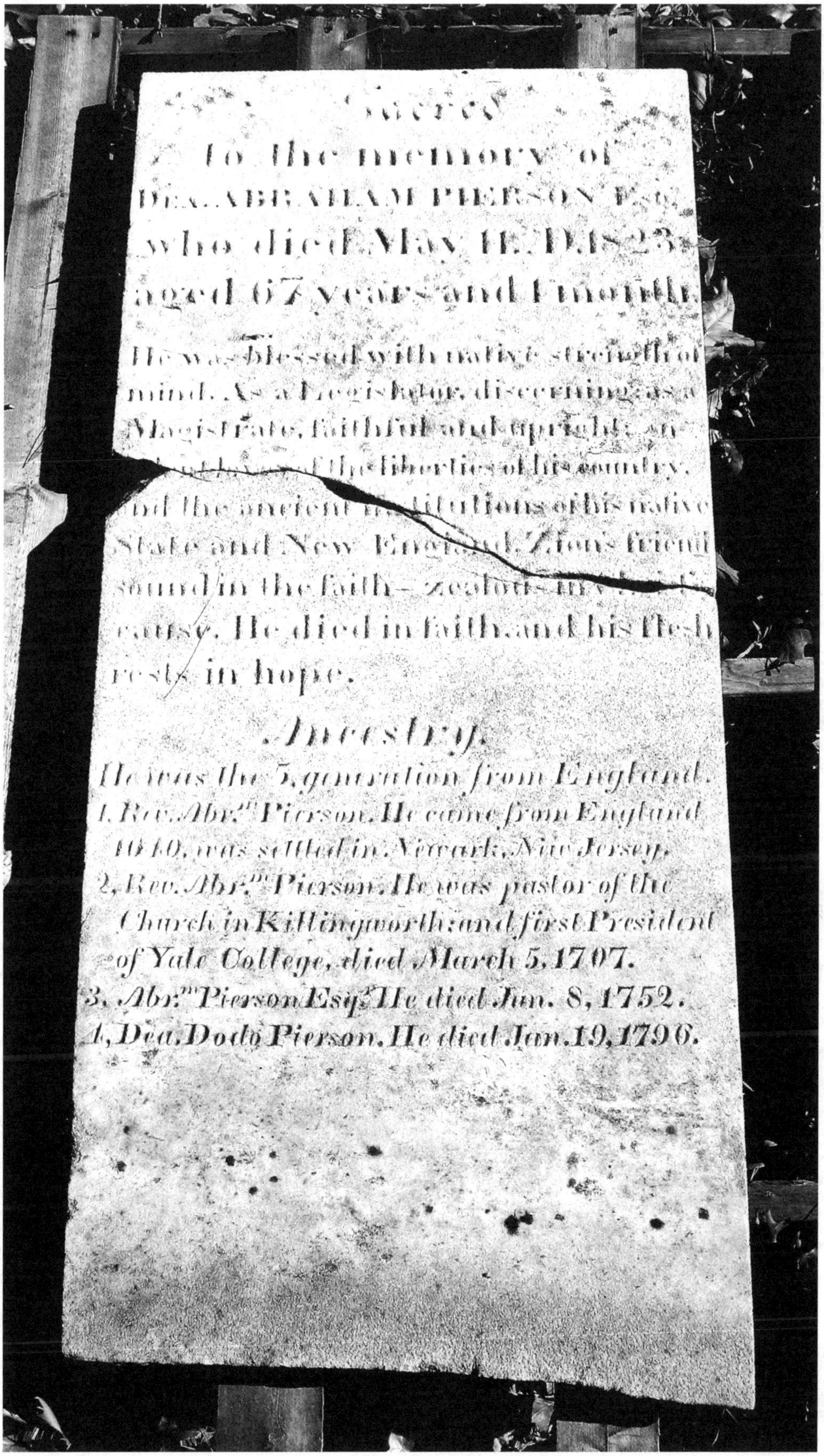

Gravestone of Abraham Pierson (1756–1823), fifth Deacon. Union District Cemetery.

Deacon Nathan Hull, 1831.
Lane District Cemetery.

Deacon John Hinckley, 1849.
Southwest District Cemetery.

Deacon Nathan Hull died in 1831 and is buried in the Lane District Cemetery. The gravestone of John Hinckley was broken but has been repaired. The second Abel Wilcox was deacon from 1831 to 1877 and was the second Superintendent of the Sabbath School. His gravestone is broken and in the Parker Hill District Cemetery. The gravestone of Heman S. Franklin who died in 1850 was found recently during the restoration of his house on Roast Meat Hill Road. It was buried near a corner of the foundation. The monument for Heman and his wife Maria, who outlived him by 38 years, is in the Union District Cemetery and may have replaced the earlier broken stone.

Deacon Abel Wilcox, 1877.
Parker Hill District Cemetery.

It may be more than coincidence that the gravestones of Deacons Pierson, Hinckley, Wilcox, and Franklin are broken. None of the breaks are recent. In 1818, members of the Society were assessed "25 Cents on the Dollar" for the expenses of building the second meetinghouse. This was an enormous tax and some were unable to pay it. In subsequent years, the Society brought legal action and in some cases possessed houses, barns, and land from those who hadn't paid their tax. It is known there was resentment as the new meetinghouse was vandalized on more than one occasion. It is possible this anger extended to the desecration of the gravestones of the deacons.

Deacon Heman S. Franklin, 1850.

Dea. Heman S., 1850, and Maria E., 1888, Franklin.
Union District Cemetery.

Deacon Julius, 1903, and Huldah, 1872, Buell.
Evergreen Cemetery.

Lauren L. Nettleton was deacon from 1854 to 1910. He was born in Killingworth in 1824, the son of Ezra Nettleton and Miriam Lane. He married Eliza C. Evarts in 1850. He considered himself a farmer and taught school in Killingworth and surrounding towns for many years. He was president of the Agricultural Society. He held town office as selectman and assessor. Besides serving as deacon, he was Superintendent of the Sabbath School in the Congregational Church.

Deacon Sherman E. Griswold, 1919.

Dea. Lauren L., 1910, and Eliza C., 1909, Nettleton.

Dea. Norman L. Parmelee, 1923, and Family.

Evergreen Cemetery.

Although not a deacon, an individual of importance to the establishment of an Episcopal Church in Killingworth should be included. The Bristols were early settlers of New Haven and East Guilford (now Madison). When a new ecclesiastical society was formed in 1753 in the northern part of East Guilford, it was named North Bristol (now North Madison) after Bezaleel Bristol (1681–1764). His son, Bezaleel (1712–1753) who settled in North Killingworth, is buried in the Pine Orchard District Cemetery. His son, also named Bezaleel (1749–1828), was a Captain of the militia in the Revolutionary War. The Bristols were instrumental in the establishment of the Episcopal Church in Killingworth. An Episcopalian Society was formed in 1800 and consisted of members from North Bristol and North Killingworth. Construction of a church began in 1803 on land belonging to Bezaleel Bristol in North Killingworth. In 1807, Bezaleel donated the land to the church.

Bezaleel Bristol Esq., 1828. Emmanuel Episcopal Church.

Thomas Lyman was a deacon in the Congregational Church in Durham. His gravestone bears the winged death's head. Deacon Henry Crane (1677–1741) was the son of Henry Crane Sr. (c1635–1711), one of the original settlers of the Hammonasset Plantation and a representative to the General Court, lieutenant of the trainband, captain of militia, and justice of the peace for New London County. Henry Crane Jr. moved to the part of Killingworth that was later set off to Durham and was one of the original 34 proprietors of Durham. He was a deacon, representative to the General Court, and justice of the peace for New Haven County. He left a large estate including a 750 acre farm.

Deacon Thomas Lyman, sandstone, 19"w x 24"h, 1725. Old Durham Cemetery.

Deacon Henry Crane, sandstone, 24 ½"w x 28"h, 1741. Old Durham Cemetery.

Gravestones of the Military

Lieut. Daniel Kelsey, 1650–1727. Kelsey Family plot, Indian River Cemetery.

Residents of Killingworth have fought in all of the wars from the first settlement to the present time. This chapter illustrates some of the markers for these veterans through the Spanish-American War. Others will be found in the chapter on the cemeteries. The graves of veterans are marked by marble patriot markers that were placed by the State of Connecticut in the 1920s. In some cases, the gravestones have disintegrated or disappeared and the patriot markers are all that remain to mark the grave.

King Philip's War. The first known veterans from Killingworth are those who fought in King Philip's War (1675–1676.) With the outbreak of the war, two fortifications were built, one at the Rev. Woodbridge's place and the other at Andrew Ward's. Although no conflicts occurred in the area, colonists from throughout New England joined in the war. It was customary at the time to reward those who served the community with grants of land. At a Town meeting on May 21, 1688 "The town by their vote granted unto those that ware out Soulders in the indian Wards to wit Nathaniell Haydon John Griswold John Hull Daniell Kellcy Joseph Hull Samuell Stevens John Shether Samuel Shether Daniell Clarke John Lee John Mentar - Six acras of Land apeace in the woods : with out the tow miles bounds : and to be tacken up in tow feailds : the one on the west-side of the indian River - and the other on the east side of the s^d river : which Lands is not to prediuce no former grants or high ways nor to hinder or debar any Coming unto or Carting from ether of the Cedar Swamps . . . ." Although some of these men are probably buried in the Indian River Cemetery, the only marker that could be found is a later one for Lieut. Daniel Kelsey (1650–1727.)

Militia. In colonial times, the militia was an important social structure, necessary to provide defense and public safety for the community. All able-bodied males were expected to be members of the local militia. The men from a town comprised a militia company known as a training band, or trainband. Companies from different towns were organized into regiments. Those in the militia were not issued arms or uniforms but brought their own weapons and wore their own farmer's clothes. The militia was required to hold training days on a regular basis in which the men practiced marksmanship and military drills. Training days were also festive events for the community that involved the entire family and provided ample food and drink for all. The local militia officers were elected by the company and appointed by the General Assembly. They were generally among the most respected or prominent men in the community. Most of the military titles, e. g., Capt., Lieut., Ens., found on Killingworth gravestones are the ranks of those who were in the militia.

John Lane was appointed by the General Assembly "Captain of the 12th company or trainband in the 7th regiment in this Colony" in May 1754. The first Training Plain in Killingworth was a flat piece of land lying between Route 81 and Green Hill Road and south of Stevens Road. In 1755, Capt. John

Lane was killed during training exercises at the Training Plain. The death was assumed to be an accident during shooting exercises, but no one ever took responsibility for the shooting. The inscription on his gravestone is very faint and is visible for only a few minutes of each day when the sun is in the optimal position.

Capt. John Lane (1708–1755). Gneiss, Union District Cemetery.

Probably the most militaristic gravestone in the area is that of Nathanael Sutlief in the Old Durham Yard. It is also one of the few in the area to be in the baroque style. Two fearsome skulls flank the base of the inscription whose oval shape resembles a shield. Crossed swords are present in the lunette beneath a crown. The epitaph reads "Shield & Spear, Let Mortal wear; Whilst I Ætherial Honour Share." Many of his ancestors were involved in military campaigns in Colonial America. His father Nathaniel Sutliff, was one of the first settlers of Durham and a representative to the General Assembly. Nathanael was Captain of the second company or trainband at West Haddam which later became a part of Durham. He was one of the founders of the circulating library in Durham, one of the first in America. He owned slaves, had large land holdings, and was the aristocrat of the family.

Capt. Nathanael Sutlief (1695–1760). Sandstone, 27"w x 54"h, Old Durham Cemetery.

French and Indian War. Peleg Redfield, fifth son of Theophilus and Priscilla Redfield, was born April 2, 1723 in Killingworth. After serving as lieutenant, he was commissioned captain of the tenth company in March, 1760 which he raised in and around Killingworth. The company, which fought in Canada, consisted of the Captain, two Lieutenants, one ensign, five Sergeants, two drummers, and 81 rank and file. Redfield served throughout the War which closed with the surrender of Montreal in September, 1760. On his return from this campaign, Capt. Redfield was taken sick of smallpox at Albany, and died on his journey home, near Stockbridge, Mass., Dec 5, 1760. His body was brought to Killingworth and buried in the Pine Orchard Cemetery on North Chestnut Hill Road. Unfortunately, the headstone has disappeared although the footstone and a patriot marker remain.

Footstone of Peleg Redfield, (1723–1760). Capt. Peleg Redfield patriot marker, 1760.
Pine Orchard District Cemetery.

Jeremiah Nettleton, 1779.
Pine Orchard District Cemetery.

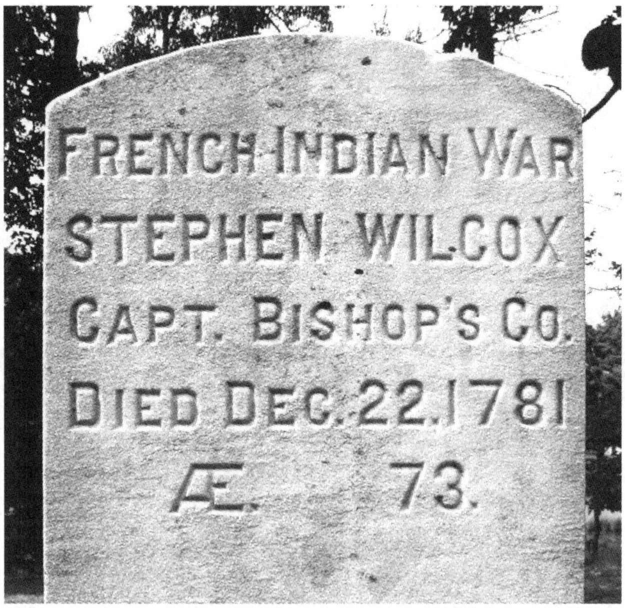

Stephen Wilcox, 1781.
Indian River Cemetery.

Revolutionary War. Killingworth was active in the Revolutionary War from the beginning. Committees of Correspondence were formed throughout the colonies to maintain communication with other towns and colonies and coordinate action against Great Britain. "At a town Meeting Holden the 13th Day of September 1774 Martonn Lord Aaron Eliot Capt Samal Crane Caleb Baldwin Capt Nathan Griswold to be a Commetty of Corespondence to Corespond with Such Other Committy as Shall be Appointed by other Towns." In April 1775, 53 men marched from Killingworth for the relief of Boston in the Lexington Alarm. Men fought throughout the Revolution, often leaving for a period of time and then returning to their farms. Besides those who fought in the war, the farmers of Killingworth supplied hay, grain, beef, and pork for the Continental Army. Women made contributions in supplying clothes, blankets, and provisions to the soldiers and caring for the sick and wounded.

Memorial for Peter Griffing, 1779. Indian River Cemetery.

John Lane, 1796. Union District Cemetery.

Capt. Aaron Kelsey, 1799. Southwest District.

Eli Kelsey, 1788. Southwest District Cemetery.

Elijah Wilcox, 1842. Southwest District Cemetery.

Capt. Bezeliel Bristol, 1828. Pine Orchard Cemetery.

Capt. Nathan Griswold, 1826. Union District Cemetery.

Joseph Lane, 1844. Lane District Cemetery.

Capt. Aaron Stevens, 1820. Union District Cemetery.

Benoni Camp died in the Battle of the Wabash in the Northwest Indian War on November 4, 1791. The battle was the most severe defeat ever suffered by the United States at the hands of American Indians. President George Washington forced General St. Clair to resign after the defeat.

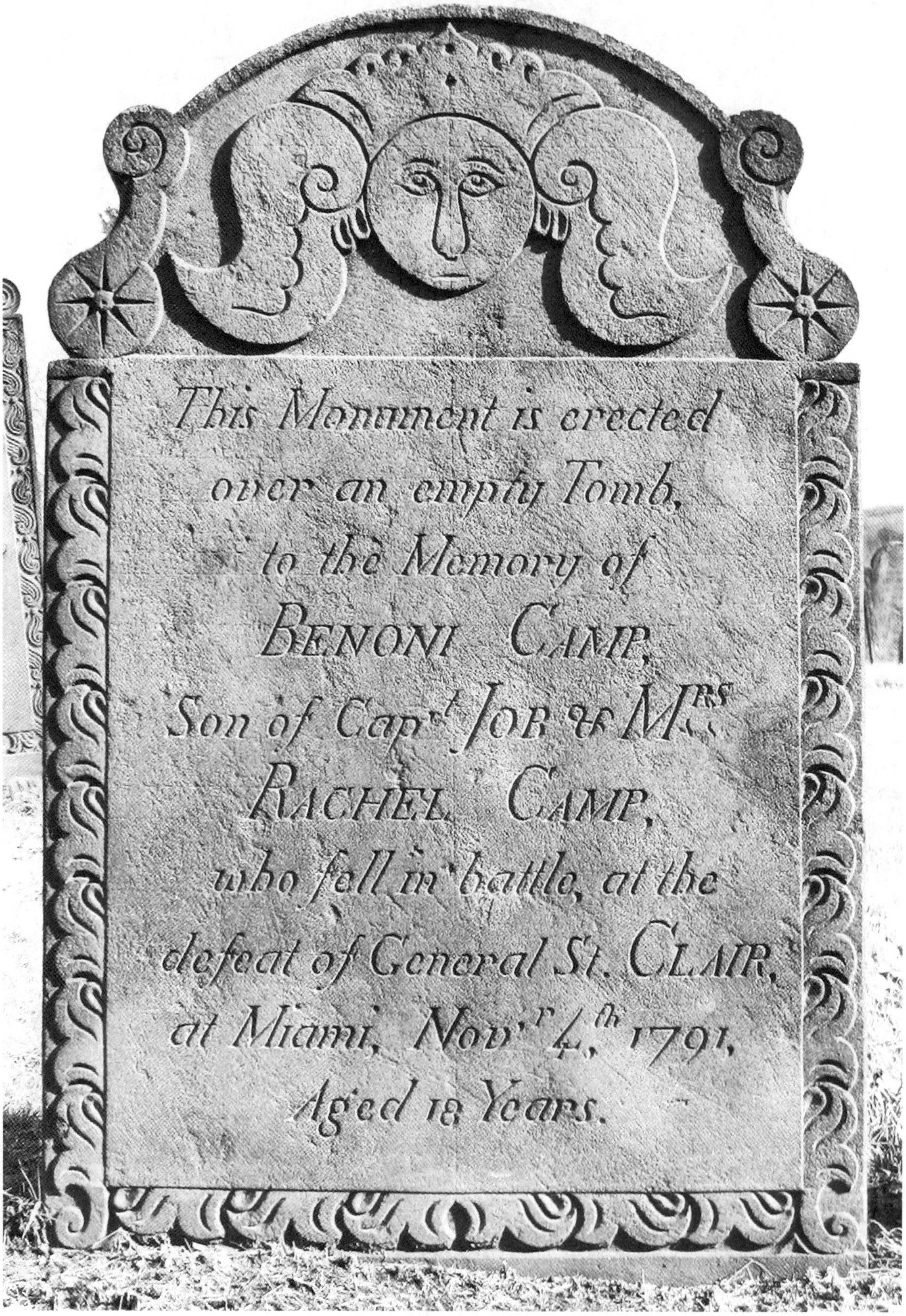

Memorial for Benoni Camp, 1791. Old Durham Cemetery.

War of 1812. During the War of 1812, Killingworth had one militia company commanded by Capt. Benjamin Hurd. Several coasting schooners were blockaded in the harbor. The British made several raids on the harbor but were repelled by the militia and citizens. Capt. Amaziah Bray commanded a company of artillery, half stationed in Saybrook and half in Killingworth. In November 1814, the men in his command drove off a British sloop of war that had forced a coasting schooner into the harbor.

Ashbel Griswold, 1830. Union District.

Civil War. In the Civil War on August 7, 1862, "Resolved, That for the purpose of encouraging enlistments under the call of the President of the United States bearing the date July 1st AD 1862 for three hundred thousand additional troops, the Town of Killingworth will pay in addition to all other bounties and compensations, the sum of one hundred Dollars to each resident of this Town who since July 1st has enlisted." The town offered a bounty of $100 to those who enlisted in order to meet its quota. Twenty one Killingworth men lost their lives in the Civil War.

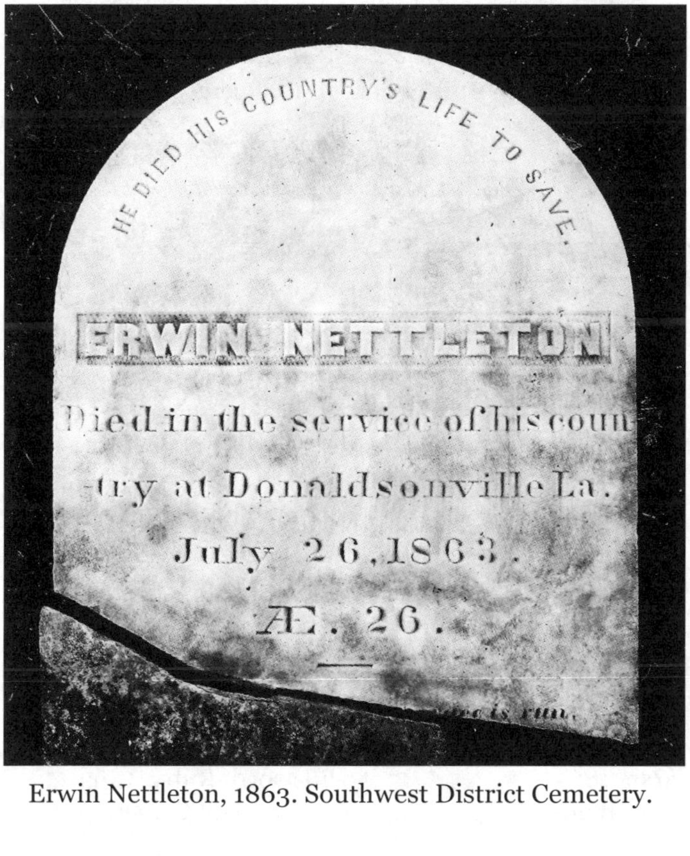

Erwin Nettleton, 1863. Southwest District Cemetery.

Elford C. Franklin, 1862. Charles Franklin, 1864. Civil War moument. Union District Cemetery.

Wm. Alfred Buell, 1862. Indian River Cemetery.

Lieut. G. Austin Chittenden, 1890. Evergreen Cemetery.

Samuel Hill, 1862.
Union District Cemetery.

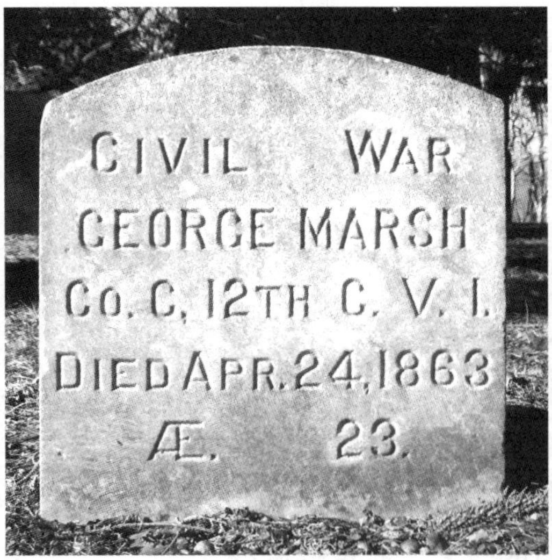

George Marsh, 1863.
Union District Cemetery.

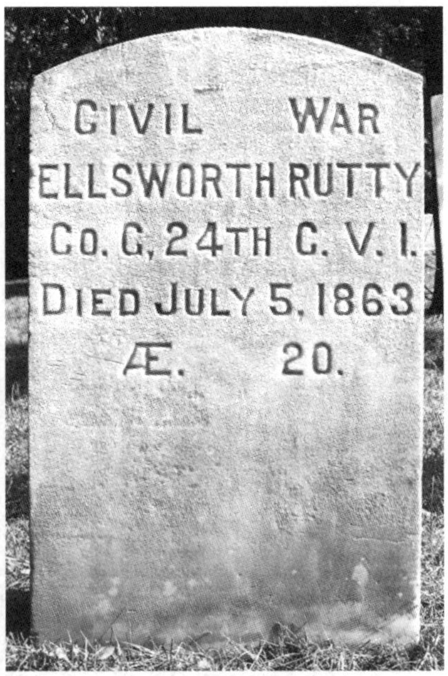

Ellsworth Rutty, 1863.
Parker Hill Cemetery.

Civil War monument surrounded by four arbor vitae trees, marble obelisk, Union District Cemetery. Henry Edgar Barnum, 1863; Elford C. Franklin, 1862; Charles Franklin, 1864; Joseph Vaill Evarts, 1863.

Spanish-American War. In the Spanish-American War (1898), the United States sought to dislodge Spain from longstanding colonial outposts in both the Caribbean and the South Pacific. A metal Spanish War Veterans marker in front of the Charles V. Parker monument reads "U.S.A., Porto Rico, Cuba, and Philippine Islands."

Charles V. Parker, 1899. Indian River Cemetery.

Causes of Death

Upon walking through the Killingworth or any other colonial cemeteries and reading the inscriptions on the gravestones, one is struck by the large number of deaths of infants, children, and young adults. Most of the early deaths were due to infectious diseases that today are controlled by adequate sanitation, vaccination, and antibiotics. Diphtheria (throat distemper) was a major cause of death in children and often resulted in multiple deaths in the same family. It is not uncommon in the Killingworth cemeteries to see gravestones of children that died within a few days of each other. Two children of Aaron and Lydia Kelsey died on the same day in 1777. Epidemics of measles resulted in high mortality. Mumps and whooping cough could be fatal. Some diseases now classified as common childhood ailments were more lethal then due to lack of immunity and effective treatment for the diseases. The causes of death are not given on gravestones, except for a few that say "died of the small pox" such as the Jared Crane and Phinehas Spelman markers. The most significant eighteenth century diseases were dysentery, caused by the bacterium *Shigella*, and typhoid fever, caused by the bacterium *Salmonella*, both spread through drinking water contaminated with human waste. Other common diseases with significant mortality rates were smallpox, tuberculosis (consumption), influenza, typhus, yellow fever, and scarlet fever. An epidemic of yellow fever occurred in New Haven in 1794. Some of these diseases were more prevalent in urban areas. Accidents were a common cause of death for all ages in Colonial America.

Parsons Still Born Son, 1777. Old Durham Cemetery.

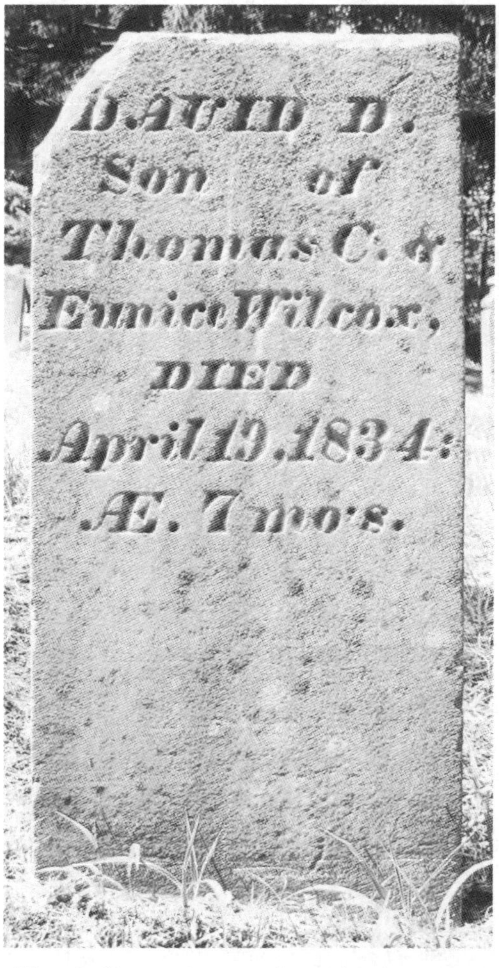

David D. Wilcox, 1834. Union District Cemetery.

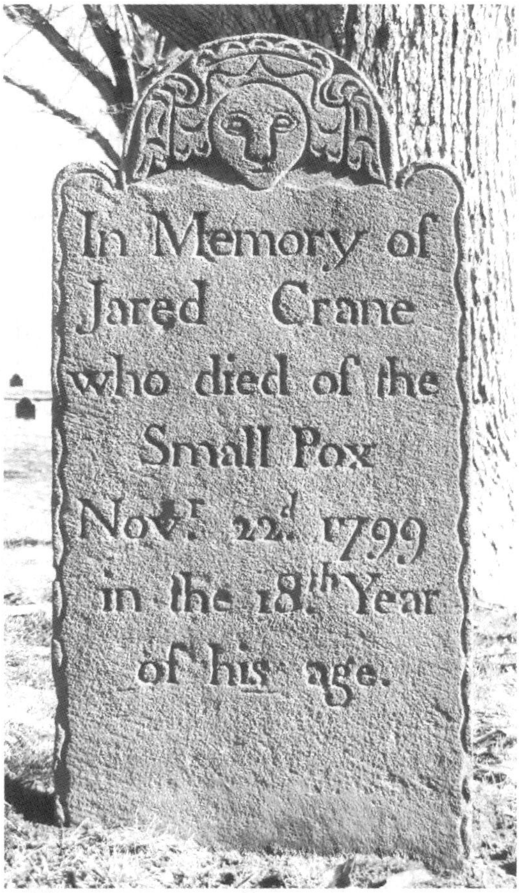

Jared Crane, 1799. Indian River Cemetery.

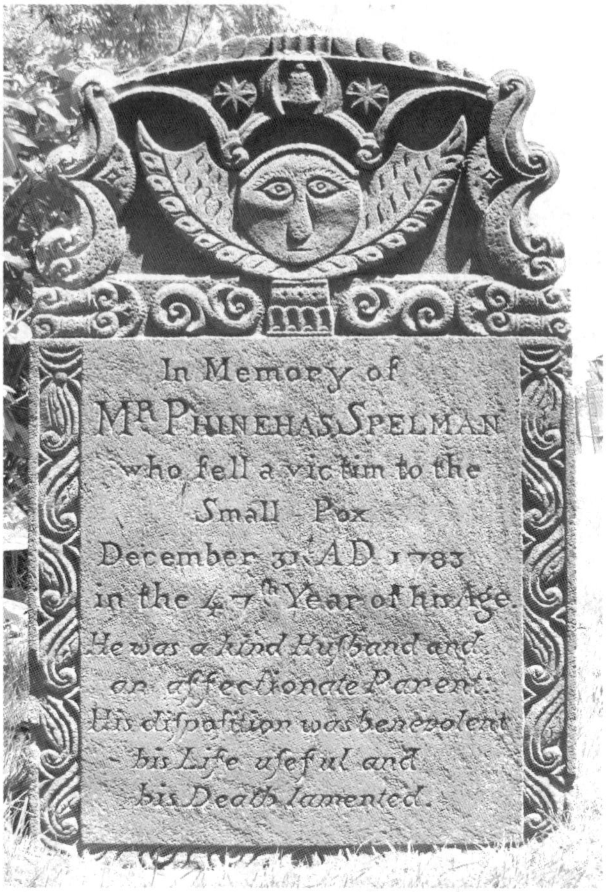

Phinehas Spelman, 1783. Old Durham Cemetery.

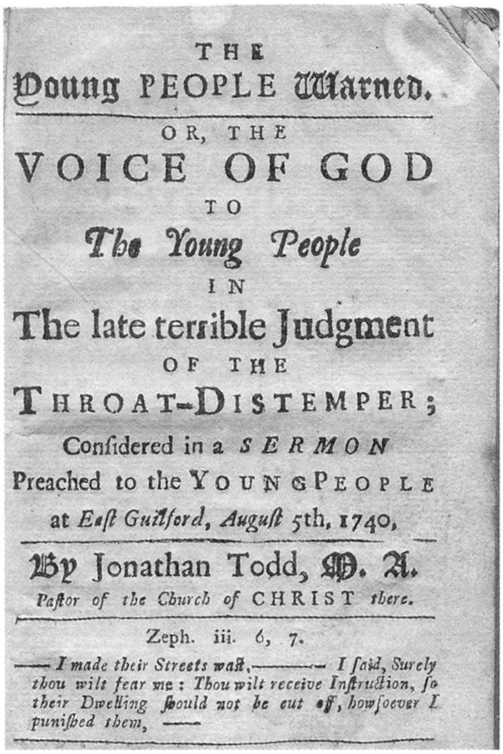
THE
Young PEOPLE Warned.
OR, THE
VOICE OF GOD
TO
The Young People
IN
The late terrible Judgment
OF THE
THROAT-DISTEMPER;
Confidered in a SERMON
Preached to the YOUNG PEOPLE
at *East Guilford, August* 5th, 1740,

By Jonathan Todd, M. A.
Paftor of the Church of CHRIST *there.*

Zeph. iii. 6, 7.
——I made their Streets waft,—— I faid, Surely thou wilt fear me: Thou wilt receive Inftruction, fo their Dwelling fhould not be cut off, howfoever I punifhed them, ——

Sermon preached by the Rev. Jonathan Todd following a death due to diphtheria.

Margery and Aaron Kelcey, September 17, 1777.
Southwest District Cemetery.

Diseases occurring in Middlesex County listed by Field (1819) were dysentery, throat distemper, typhus fever, yellow fever, and consumption. He states that a "long-fever" prevailed in North Killingworth in 1751 and 1752. The long fever was probably typhoid fever. Scarlet fever was in North Killingworth in 1784.

Some families lost most of their children. It has been said that parents in colonial times tried not to become too attached to their children until they reached at least the age of five. This is doubtful and they certainly grieved as much for lost children as one would today. However, they also retained the Puritan ethic that death was inevitable and that God gave them the children and could also take them back. Because of their spiritual beliefs, they may have been better able to accept the loss of their children.

Another significant cause of death was complications resulting from childbirth. There are many gravestones of young women in Killingworth cemeteries. There often can be found nearby the gravestone of an infant who died around the same time as the mother. The inscription on the Mary Wilcox marker includes an infant son.

Mary Wilcox and infant son, 1814.
Union District Cemetery.

Capt. Samuel and Julia Kelsey, 1800.
Indian River Cemetery.

Other causes of death were accidents, shipwrecks, and war. Michael Griswold Jr. was killed by a falling beam during a house raising in 1771. The Rev. William Seward preached two sermons on the death that were published. The sermons preached on the death of persons in the eighteenth century were not pleasant eulogies on the deceased person's life and virtues. Instead, they were stern warnings to the living to give up their sinful ways and accept the Lord before they suffered the same fate. Samuel Kelsey died at sea in 1800. Twenty one Killingworth men died in the Civil War.

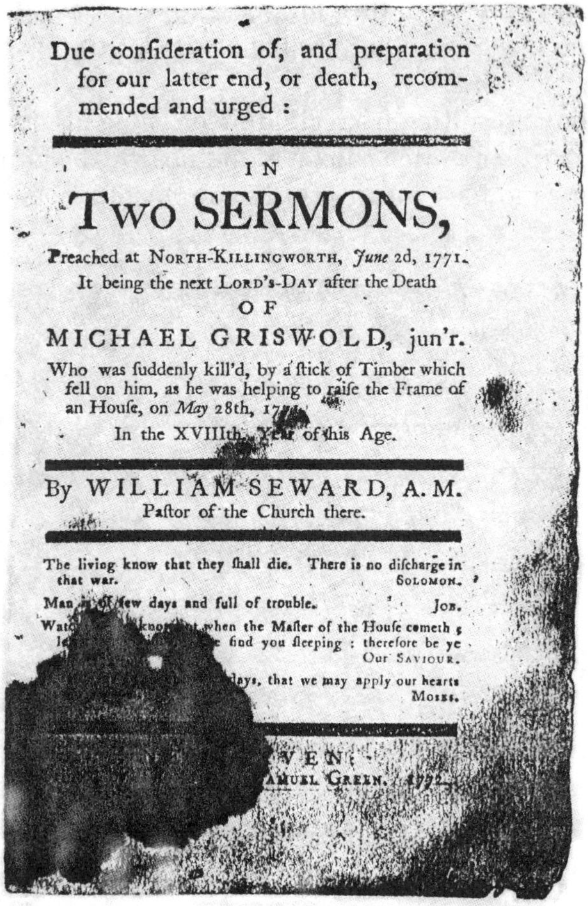

Due confideration of, and preparation for our latter end, or death, recommended and urged :

IN

Two SERMONS,

Preached at NORTH-KILLINGWORTH, *June* 2d, 1771.
It being the next LORD's-DAY after the Death
OF
MICHAEL GRISWOLD, jun'r.
Who was fuddenly kill'd, by a ftick of Timber which fell on him, as he was helping to raife the Frame of an Houfe, on *May* 28th, 17[illegible]
In the XVIIIth [illegible] of his Age.

By WILLIAM SEWARD, A.M.
Paftor of the Church there.

The living know that they fhall die. There is no difcharge in that war. SOLOMON.

Man [illegible] few days and full of trouble. JOB.

Wat[illegible] know[illegible] when the Mafter of the Houfe cometh [illegible] find you fleeping : therefore be ye [illegible] OUR SAVIOUR.

[illegible] days, that we may apply our hearts [illegible] MOSES.

[illegible] VEN: [illegible] AMUEL GREEN. 1772.

Sermons preached by the Rev. William Seward on the death of Michael Griswold from a falling beam, 1771.

Wilson S. Hall, 1862. Union District Cemetery.

In 1927, Earl Kelsey and his wife recorded the names and ages of death on the gravestones in the Union District Cemetery, almost all of which are from the eighteenth and nineteenth centuries. This list of about 400 markers is the earliest known record of the gravestones in the cemetery. Some gravestones were unreadable at that time and many more have deteriorated or disappeared since then. There are also a large number of unmarked graves in the cemetery for which there is no data. Using the information from Kelsey's list, a graph was prepared of ages at time of death for men and women. The graph shows the expected high mortality of infants and young children. It is unknown why there were many more deaths for young males than females, unless the graves of the latter were not always marked with headstones. There were more women than men dying in their late teens, twenties and thirties, mainly due to complications of childbirth. The difference would be even greater except that the numbers for men include seven men in this cemetery, mostly in their twenties, who died in the Civil War. More men died in their sixties than women. Contrary to common notion, once past childhood, the majority of people had normal life spans with many living into their seventies, eighties, and nineties.

Deaths of Men and Women by Age. Union District Cemetery

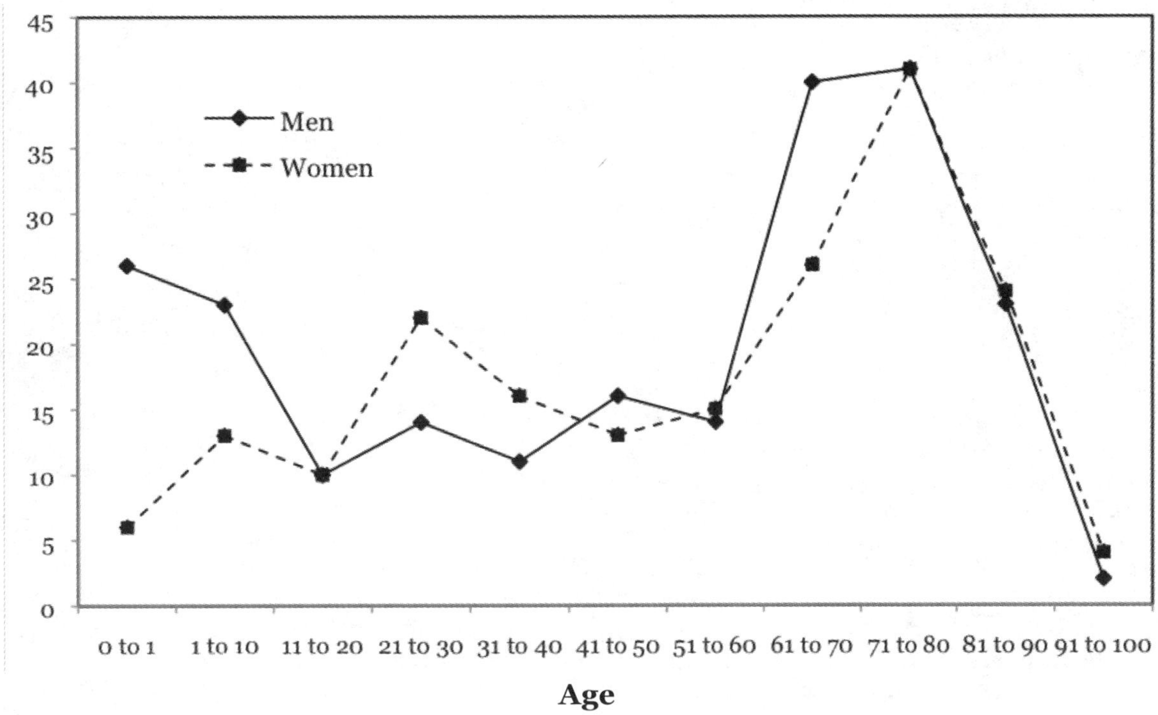

In the second half of the nineteenth century the major causes of death in Killingworth were consumption (tuberculosis), typhoid fever, dysentery, apoplexy (stroke), and "old age." By that time, more was known about diseases and many more were listed. Causes of death for infants and children included stillborn, premature birth, malformation, hydrocephalus, marasmus (malnutrition), diphtheria, pertussis (whooping cough), croup, and scarlet fever. Infectious diseases were common and included pneumonia, la grippe (influenza), brain fever (encephalitis), bilious fever, childbed fever (puerperal fever), metritis, phthisis (tuberculosis), scrofula (tuberculosis), bronchitis, pleurisy, gastritis, inflammation of bowels, meningitis, cholera, lock jaw (tetanus), erysipelas, typhus fever, variola (smallpox), diarrhea, malarial fever, and worms. Other causes of death were asthma, hernia, hemorrhage, epilepsy, Bright's disease (nephritis), convulsions, insanity, and suicide. Accidents remained common and death records list accidents, injury, fracture, lightning, burned, scalded, fall separating spinal cord, gun shot wound in neck, railroad accident, and drowning as causes of death. There is greater mention of chronic and degenerative diseases affecting older people including cancer, diabetes, cirrhosis, stroke, heart disease, cardiac failure, dropsy, jaundice, rheumatism, kidney disease, gangrene, paralysis, senility, and debility.

The record for longevity in the Killingworth area is that of Elisabeth Tooley. She died in 1757 at the age of 107 and is buried in the Indian River Cemetery. She married Christopher (Christando) Tooley (1650–1717/18) in 1683 and together they had ten children in Killingworth. Her lifetime spanned over half of the existence of Colonial America.

Elisabeth Tooley (1650–1757). Indian River Cemetery.

Burial and Funeral Practices

The Puritans had little regard for the physical body after death, and they did not dwell on memorials or public expressions of grief even though they may have mourned in private. They also rejected the practice of churchyard burials and graveside prayers as Papist influences. Instead, the towns set aside land as common community burial grounds. In the earliest colonial days, a body was carried to its final resting place on a frame of planks. The first colonists were buried without coffins. By the 1700s, people were hiring carpenters and cabinetmakers to make coffins. During the nineteenth century, coffin making became a full-time business and coffin shops were established. In the second half of the nineteenth century, caskets, which were more elaborate than coffins came into use. The caskets were made of metals or woods and lined with various materials including satin. Embalming came into use during the Civil War, which involved many servicemen dying far from home, and their families wishing them returned for local burial. Cremation was not practiced in America until the end of the nineteenth century.

In Killingworth in the eighteenth and nineteenth centuries, a person was paid by the town for digging a grave in the town graveyards.

> December 15, 1788. To Mr. Abraham Turner for opening 2 Graves, 4*s*.
> December 13, 1791. to Capt Bezaleel Bristol for opening one grave, 2*s*.
> November 8, 1819. To Edward Lane for opening 4 graves at 44 Cents each, $1.76.
> September 30, 1896. Almon Nettleton Digging & filling grave for J. L. Chatfield, $3.50.

The Killingworth graveyards are located in soft sand that made digging easier. Families tended to be buried together in family plots.

In the earlier burials, the bodies were buried with the head to the west and the feet to the east in the belief that at the cock's crow on judgment day, the resurrected body would arise from the grave to face the rising sun. The headstone and the footstone were set with carved surfaces facing away from the grave so that visitors would not have to stand on the grave to read the inscriptions. Thus, usually the headstones face west and footstones face east.

By the eighteenth century, the stern practices of the early Puritans had been eased. In Colonial Killingworth, funerals were held at the church or in private homes. The pastor gave a sermon and prayers were said. Some of the eighteenth and nineteenth century funeral sermons given in Killingworth were published. The church bell was rung at the decease of persons. The funeral procession moved from the meetinghouse to the burying ground. The deceased was carried in a horse drawn cart or wagon, later a hearse. The pastor followed in a carriage. Families and friends followed in carts, on horseback, or on foot. The mourners were dressed in black. Some of the burying grounds like the Union District Cemetery have a central aisle for the procession to enter. At the burying ground, more orations and prayers were read. After the burial, the family often conducted an open house where large quantities of food and drink were provided.

The first hearses were open horse drawn wagons. These could be painted black and have a top but were usually devoid of ornamentation. It is likely this was the first type of hearse used in Killingworth. The first true hearse carriages had a plain chassis but could have ornaments such as urns or wooden torches with eternal flames on top. By the middle of the nineteenth century, the appearance of the hearse began to change. They became larger and considerably more ornate with fancy gilded carvings and glass windows with draperies inside. This was the type of hearse purchased by the Town of Killingworth in 1871.

The first record of a hearse in Killingworth is a document entitled "Reccord of the herse Meetting 1854 & 55." This document contains the minutes of meetings of the inhabitants of the Lane District regarding a hearse. At a meeting held in the Lane District schoolhouse on March 13, 1854, Deacon Abel Wilcox was appointed moderator, Wyllys D. Kelsey clerk, and Jared Rutty collector. At the meeting, it was "Voted that we appoint a Committee of two individuals to enter into contract with some person to place upon the hearse a suitable top the expense not to exceed 25 dollars. Also to ascertain where a suitable site can be had on which to erect a house for the hearse . . . ."

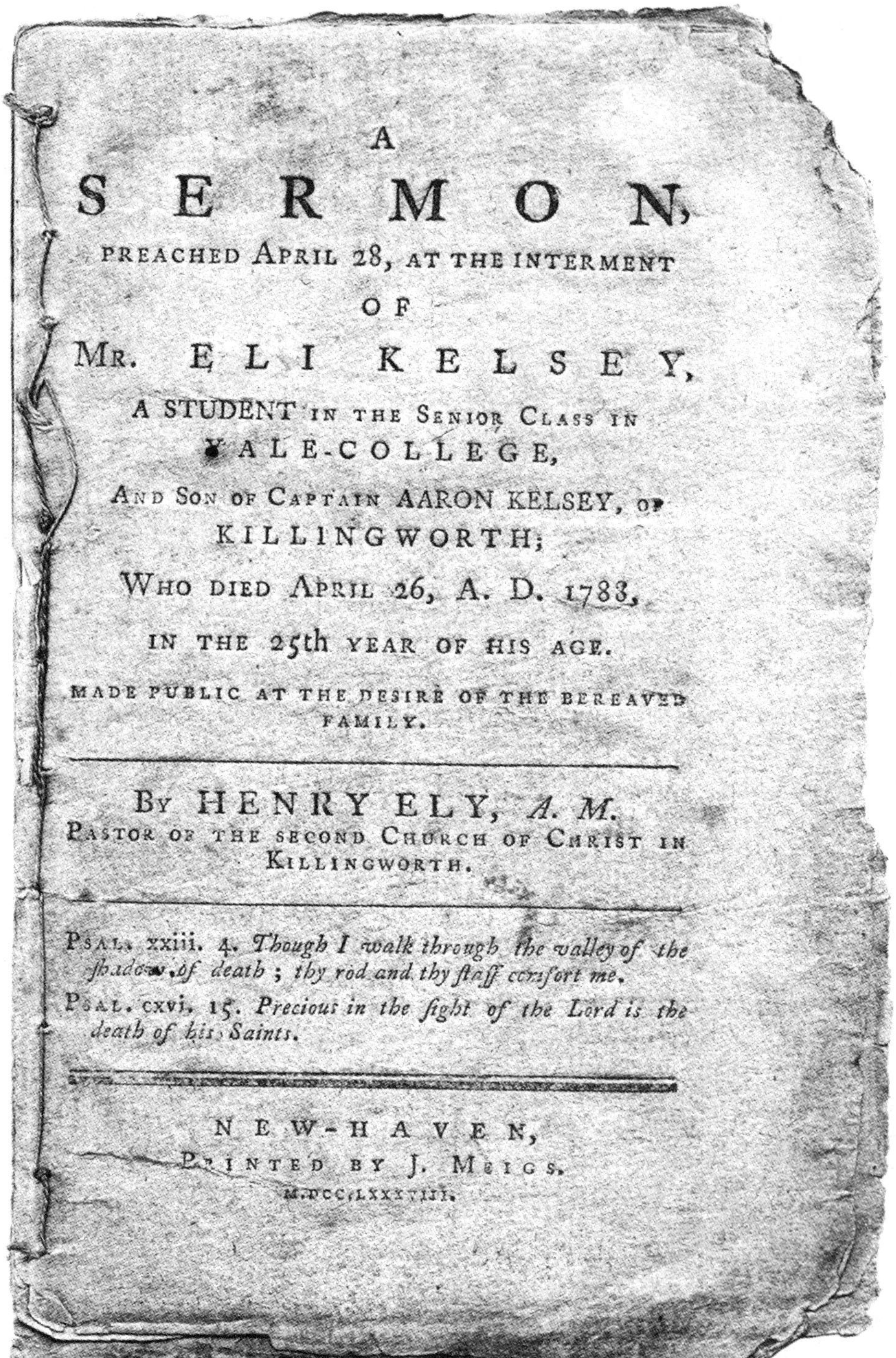

A
SERMON,
PREACHED APRIL 28, AT THE INTERMENT
OF
MR. ELI KELSEY,
A STUDENT IN THE SENIOR CLASS IN
YALE-COLLEGE,
AND SON OF CAPTAIN AARON KELSEY, OF
KILLINGWORTH;
WHO DIED APRIL 26, A. D. 1788,
IN THE 25th YEAR OF HIS AGE.
MADE PUBLIC AT THE DESIRE OF THE BEREAVED FAMILY.

BY HENRY ELY, *A. M.*
PASTOR OF THE SECOND CHURCH OF CHRIST IN KILLINGWORTH.

PSAL. xxiii. 4. *Though I walk through the valley of the shadow of death ; thy rod and thy staff comfort me.*
PSAL. cxvi. 15. *Precious in the sight of the Lord is the death of his Saints.*

NEW-HAVEN,
PRINTED BY J. MEIGS.
M.DCC.LXXXVIII.

Sermon preached by the Rev. Henry Ely at the interment of Eli Kelsey, April 28, 1788.

Based on this vote, the Lane District owned a hearse. It was probably little more than an open wagon in view of the vote to put a top on it. At the next meeting in April, the committee reported that they had contracted with Mr. Alfred Norton to put a top on the hearse for $23. It was voted to put the hearse house "on the corner west of the Meeting house" and to circulate subscription papers to raise funds for the hearse house.

They must not have been able to obtain the desired site because at a meeting on September 11, 1854, it was "Voted that we reconsider the vote to set the Herse House on the corner west of the meeting house. Voted that we set the Herse House in the north west corner of the burying ground in the eastern part of the district." The Lane and Parker Hill School Districts had been combined as the Lane District, so that the burying ground referred to is the Parker Hill Cemetery. It is not known if a hearse house was built at this cemetery.

The final entry in the document records that at the annual School Meeting in the Lane District on September 25, 1855, Edward Rutty was appointed to take charge of the hearse. It was also "Voted that the person who has charg of the herse may hire the herse to any person out of the district and to appropriate the avails to the repairs of the herse." Thus, the hearse could be rented out.

Besides the Lane District hearse, the Congregational Society (Second Ecclesiastical Society) owned a hearse, and it is possible other school districts had hearses. These hearses may not have been readily available to all residents. In 1871, a petition was presented to the town requesting that the town appoint an agent to procure a hearse for the use of the town. A special town meeting was held on June 12, 1871, and the following resolution was presented.

> "Resolved 1st That the public convenience and wants require that the town provide a hearse for the burial of the dead;
>
> Therefore be it,
> Resolved 2d, That Henry Kelsey and Nathan Lane be appointed agents of the town to procure such a hearse as may seem to them that the wants of the town require and provide a suitable place to house the same, provided that the whole expense to the town does not exceed five hundred Dollars."
>
> Resolved 3d, That the aforesaid agents be required to present their bills to the Selectmen of the town to be audited and approved, and when so approved the Selectmen be required to give them an order on the Treasurer of the Town for the amount so approved.
>
> Resolved 4th, That if there be not sufficient money in the treasury to meet the bills as approved, that the Selectmen of the town borrow so much money on the credit of the town as may be necessary, not to exceed the amount provided in the second Resolution.

The resolutions passed by a vote of 35 yeas and 27 nays.

Then it was "Voted, That Orlando E. Redfield have the care and charge of the hearse after it is procured, and keep it in order for use and present his bill to the Selectman for payment."

Henry Kelsey and Nathan Lane traveled to Middletown and purchased a used hearse. The hearse was made around 1860 by Cornwall & Warner Carriages. The hearse is ten feet long and seven feet in height, with glass windows on the sides and back curtained in velvet. It has a pair a carriage lamps set into brackets beside the driver's seat. The head of the casket fit under the seat of the driver. It may have been drawn by one horse but apparently this was not sufficient because in 1881 it was voted that the town provide a two horse pole for the hearse. In 1904, the selectmen appointed Lauren A. Nettleton "Driver of Town Hearse."

Regarding the housing of the hearse, on November 6, 1871, the Congregational Society voted "That we give the "Society hearse house" and the old hearse to the Committee appointed by the town to provide a suitable place in which to keep the new hearse, and that committee apply it, or its avails, towards making or providing the suitable place as contemplated by the town vote." A hearse house, probably not the original, stood behind the Congregational Church near the Agricultural Hall (Old Town Hall). The hearse house burned down in 2004.

The town donated the hearse to the Killingworth Historical Society in 1972. In 2003, the hearse was restored by Mary Lightner of Wagonland Barn, Bernardston, Massachusetts at a cost of $11,000. The repair included restoration of the detailed leatherwork on the seat and back, the interior curtains and accessories, and the frame and floor. The hearse is drawn at the annual Killingworth Memorial Day Parade and exhibited occasionally by the Historical Society.

The Killingworth Town Hearse.

In the seventeenth and eighteenth centuries, epidemics of communicable diseases often decimated communities and wiped out entire families. One of the most feared diseases was smallpox. In response, some communities operated a pest house, or house of pestilence. The pest house was a "hospital" where sick people were placed to be quarantined, die, and be buried nearby. The Town of Durham operated a pest house between 1760 and 1790. In 1759, John Jones age 47, his wife Hannah age 42, and daughter Sarah age 10 died of smallpox. It was probably because of this unfortunate event that the town decided to take action. On April 14, 1760, it was voted at a town meeting "that some house be forthwith built and erected in some suitable place, for the reception of such persons as shall be taken with infectious diseases." The pest house was located in an extremely remote area west of Cream Pot Road. The site is still remote and not easily reached but is encroached upon by a subdivision. Fortunately, the Town of Durham has obtained the site so that it will remain protected.

All that remains is a foundation with a fieldstone cellar hole. Nearby is a single brown sandstone gravestone for Timothy Hall who died with the small pox in 1771. However, there are several fieldstones in the ground that undoubtedly mark the graves of children or those too poor to afford a gravestone.

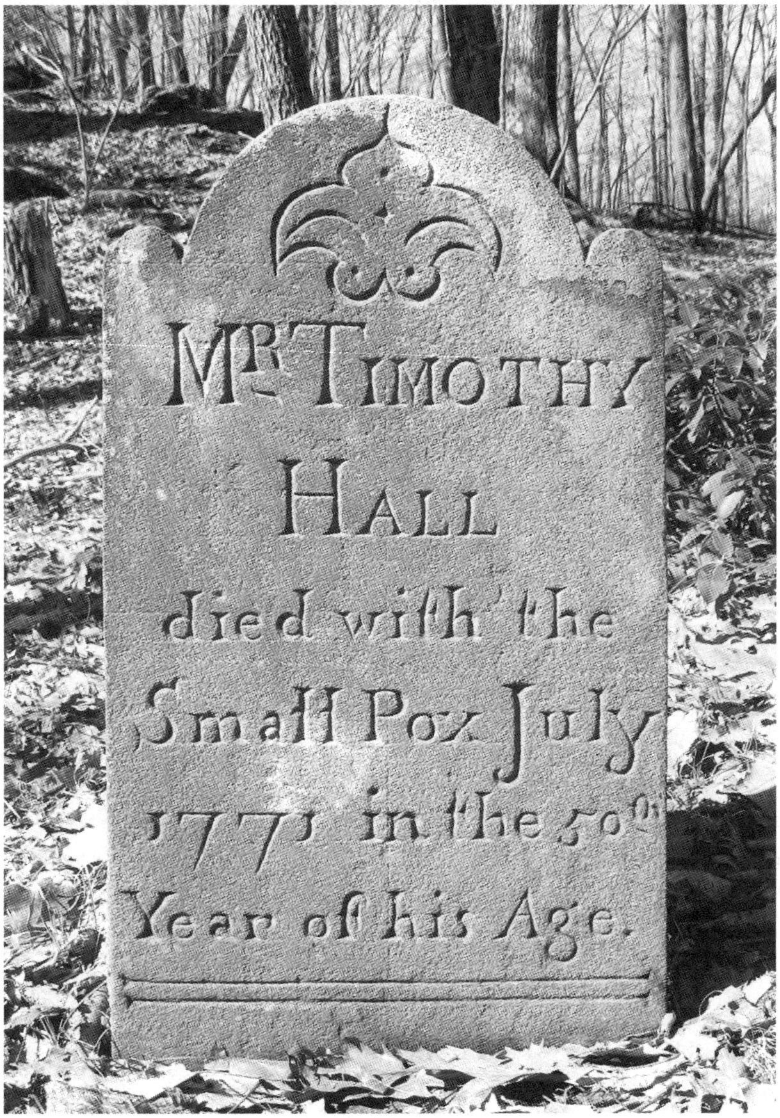

Timothy Hall, 1771, Durham Pest House.

Most towns in the area had a pest house. Dr. Benjamin Gale, who studied under his father-in-law Jared Eliot, performed inoculations for smallpox at a pest house on Duck Island off the coast of Westbrook in the 1760s. Pest houses in Guilford and Madison are still standing, although in altered form. In 1792, the town of Killingworth granted "Doctor Aaron Eliot permission to inoculate for the small pox at the Pest House in the First Society (Clinton) at the Gulf and Doctor Richard Ely permission to inoculate for the small pox at the Pest House in the North Society (present Killingworth) near Noah Kelcey's dwelling house." Those inoculated for smallpox were quarantined for three weeks at the pest house so as not to infect others. When Edward Jenner introduced vaccination for smallpox using cowpox in 1796, pest houses fell out of use.

References

Balestracci, Susan Reischmann. 1967. *Hommonossit Plantation a history of Clinton, Connecticut.* The Quarters Press, Guilford, CT, 176pp.

Barbour, Lucius B. [1924] 1996. *Vital Records of Killingworth, Connecticut 1668–1852. Births, Deaths, Marriages from the Barbour Collection.* Reprint, Golden West Genealogy, Temple City, CA, 143pp. http://www.newhorizonsgenealogicalservices.com/barbour-collection.htm

Beers, J. B. 1884. *History of Middlesex County, Connecticut, With Biographical Sketches of Its Prominent Men.* J. B. Beers & Co., New York, 579pp.

[Brooks, William E.] 1868. *Two Hundredth Anniversary of the Clinton Congregational Church, Held in Clinton, Conn., November 13th, 1867.* Tuttle, Morehouse & Taylor, New Haven, 54pp.

[Catalog.] 1859. *Catalog of the Congregational Church in Clinton, Conn., From Its Organization, in the Year 1667. To Which is Prefixed The Articles of Faith and Covenant, and also, A Sketch of the History of the Church &c.* J. H. Benham, New Haven, 35pp.

Chernack, Paulette and Cassandra Davidson. 2016. *Lasting Impressions. Art, Symbolism, and History Found in Graveyards and Cemeteries.* Peter E. Randall Publisher, Portsmouth, NH, 170pp.

Colonial Connecticut Records, The Public Records of the Colony of Connecticut, 1636-1776. University of Connecticut Libraries. https://lib.uconn.edu/find/collections/unique-collections/public-records-of-the-colony-of-connecticut-1636-1776/

Congregational Church (Second Ecclesiastical Society) Records, Killingworth, Connecticut, 1735–1893. Five volumes, Photostat copy, Original records in Connecticut State Library, Hartford, 1933.
Vol. II. Memoranda, 1782–1855; Members, 1737; Admissions, 1738–1851; Dismissions, 1834–1851; Baptisms, 1738–1850; Baptisms by Pastors of Other Churches, 1740–1811; Baptisms of Persons Belonging to Other Churches, 1782–1809; Persons Owning the Covenant, 1738–1800; Marriages, 1739–1851; Marriages by Abraham Pierson, Justice of the Peace, 1790–1814; Deaths, 1782–1851; Votes of the Church, 1785–1850.

Connecticut Gravestone Network. http://ctgravestones.org

Farber, Jessie Lie. 2003. *Early American Gravestones. Introduction to the Farber Gravestone Collection.* American Antiquarian Society. http://www.davidrumsey.com/farber/index.html

Forbes, Harriette Merrifield. 1927. *Gravestones of Early New England And the Men who made them 1653-1800.* Houghton Mifflin Co., Boston, 141pp.

Field, David. D. 1819. *A Statistical Account of the County of Middlesex in Connecticut.* Connecticut Academy of Arts and Sciences, Clark & Lyman, Middletown, 154pp.

Griswold, Glenn E. 1936. *Middlesex County Connecticut Inscriptions. Killingworth and Clinton.* Reprint, Higginson Book Co., Salem, MA, 122pp.

Hale, Charles R. 1932-1935. Hale Collection of Connecticut Cemetery Records. Connecticut Cemetery Inscriptions and Records. Middlesex County Cemetery Records. http://www.hale-collection.com/middlesex.htm

Keister, Douglas. 2004. *Stories in Stone. A Field Guide to Cemetery Symbolism and Iconography.* Gibbs Smith Publisher, Salt Lake City, 288pp.

Kelsey, Mr. & Mrs. Earl L. 1927. *A List of the Grave Markers (Head Stones) in Union District Cemetery Killingworth Connecticut.* Typewritten manuscript, Killingworth Historical Society. 21pp.

Killingworth, Town of. 1663–1747. Town Records. Miscellaneous Town Records. Manuscript Copy Made by Colonel Aaron Eliot and Abraham Pierson. Town Hall, Killingworth, Connecticut.
——. Records. Vol. 1. 1663–1703.
——. Town Records. Vol. 2. 1678–1847.
——. Town Meetings. Vol. 1. 1678–1740.
——. Town Meetings. Vol. 2. 1740–1813.

——. Proprietors Book. 1734–1795. Town Meetings. 1813–1834.
——. Town Meetings. Vol. 3. 1834–1872.
——. Town Meetings. Vol. 4. 1872–1950.

Lentz, Thomas L. 2004. *A Photographic History of Killingworth*. Killingworth Historical Society, 131pp.
——. 2007. *History of The Congregational Church in Killingworth, Connecticut*. Gateway Press, Baltimore. 181pp.
——. 2017. *Timeline of the History of Killingworth, Connecticut 1600-2017*. Killingworth Historical Society, 36pp.

Ludwig, Allan I. 1996. *Graven Images. New England Stonecarving and its Symbols, 1650–1815*. Wesleyan University Press, Middletown, Connecticut, 482pp.

Miller, Patricia A. 1988. *Connecticut 18th Century Epitaphs. Language. Love. History*. Connecticut Gravestones, 87pp.

Miller, Rev. William. 1870. *Historical Discourse of the Congregational Church in Killingworth, Connecticut, May 31, 1870*. Hoggson & Robinson, New Haven, 67pp.

Pierce, Henry. 1961. *Colonial Killingworth. A History of Clinton and Killingworth*. Clinton Historical Society, 30pp.

Slater, James A. 1987. *The Colonial Burying Grounds of Eastern Connecticut and the Men Who Made Them*. Memoirs of the Connecticut Academy of Arts & Sciences, Vol. XXI, July 1987, Archon Books, Hamden CT, 326pp.

Slater, James A., ed. 1991. *The Papers of Dr. Ernest Caulfield on Connecticut Carvers and their Work*. Markers VIII, Association for Gravestone Studies, Worcester, MA, 342pp.

Smith, Sandra E. 1986. *Vital Statistics From Church Records of The Congregational Church in Killingworth*. Typewritten manuscript, The Congregational Church in Killingworth.

Strangstad, Lynette 1995. *A Graveyard Preservation Primer*. American Association for State and Local History Book Series, AltaMira Press, New York, 126pp.

Tashjian, Dickran and Ann. 1974. *Memorials for Children of Change. The Art of Early New England Stonecarving*. Wesleyan Univ. Press, Middletown, CT, 309pp.

Thoms, Herbert. 1967. *Jared Eliot, Minister, Doctor, Scientist, And His Connecticut*. The Shoe String Press, Inc., Hamden, CT, 156pp.

Walling, H. F. 1859. *Map of Middlesex County Connecticut*. H. & C. T. Smith & Co., New York.

Yalom, Marilyn. 2008. *The American Resting Place. Four Hundred Years of History Through Our Cemeteries and Burial Grounds*. Houghton Mifflin Co., Boston, New York, 336pp.

Subject Index[1]

[1]Names of persons in the subject index are limited to pastors and historical personages.

Gravestone Index[1]

[1]Index to photographs of whole gravestones. Spelling of names is as on the gravestone.